Sir Roger de Coverley and the Spectator's Club

By

Sir Richard Steele Joseph Addison

Published by Forgotten Books 2012

Originally Published 1908

PIBN 1000517112

CASSELL'S NATIONAL LIBRARY

SIR ROGER DE COVERLEY

AND THE SPECTATOR'S CLUB

CASSELL'S NATIONAL LIBRARY.

88. Addison—Criticisms on Milton.
54.   „   Essays and Tales.
84. Bacon's Advancement of Learning.
42.   „   Essays.
65.   „   Wisdom of the Ancients.
51. Boccaccio—Tales from the Decameron.
92. Browne's Religio Medici.
4. Browning's Poems (Selection). Intro. A. D. INNES.
60. Bunyan, John—Grace Abounding.
92. Bunyan's Pilgrim's Progress. Intro. G. K. CHESTERTON.
67. Burke's Essays on the Sublime and Beautiful.
51. Burke's Thoughts on the Present Discontents.
20. Burns's Poems (Selection). Intro. NEIL MUNRO.
40. Byron (Lord)—Childe Harold's Pilgrim.
5. Carlyle—On Heroes and Hero Worship.
35.   „   On Burns and Scott.
47.   „   Sartor Resartus. Intro. G. K. CHESTERTON.
90.   „   Essays on Goethe.
Cicero—Old Age and Friendship.
Cowper's Table Talk.
95.   „   The Task.
6. Dickens (Charles)—A Christmas Carol and The Chimes.
31.   „   „   The Cricket on the Hearth.
54.   „   „   The Battle of Life.
64. Dryden's Poems.
1. Eliot (George)—Silas Marner. Intro. STUART J. REID.
17. Emerson's Essays (Selection). Intro. C. LEWIS HIND.
9. Evelyn's Diary—(The Reign of Charles II.). Intro. AUSTIN DOBSON.
96. Franklin, Autobiography of.
73. Goethe—Sorrows of Werter.
7. Goldsmith—The Vicar of Wakefield. Intro. Sir HENRY IRVING.
19. Goldsmith's Plays.
46. Hakluyt's Discovery of Muscovy.
25. Hawthorne's (Nathaniel) Tales. Intro. FRANK MATHEW.
62. Hazlitt's Essays. Intro. HERBERT PAUL.
10. Johnson's Rasselas. [PAUL.
99. Keats' Endymion.
56. Lamb, Charles—Essays of Elia. Intro. WILLIAM ARCHER.
87. Locke's Civil Government.
24. Macaulay's Lays of Ancient Rome.
38.   „   Warren Hastings.
50.   „   Burleigh, &c.
77.   „   Clive.
94.   „   Chatham, &c.
59. Marco Polo—Voyages and Travels.
85. Maundeville's Travels.
36. Milton's Paradise Lost—I.
37.   „   „   II.
57.   „   Areopagitica.
70.   „   Earlier Poems.
86.   „   Paradise Regained.
43. More (Sir Thomas)—Utopia.
15. Poe's (Edgar Allan) Tales—(Selection). Intro. TIGHE HOPKINS.
98. Pope's Essay on Man.

109. Ruskin—Unto this Last. Intro. J. A. HOBSON.
110.   „   The Two Paths. Intro. GRAHAM WALLAS.
111.   „   The Political Economy of Art. Intro. C. F. G. MASTERMAN, M.P.
16. Scott (Sir Walter)—The Lady of the Lake.
28.   „   „   „   Marmion. [Lake.
81.   „   „   „   The Lay of the Last Minstrel.
34. Shakespeare—A Midsummer Night's Dream.
61.   „   A Winter's Tale.
100.   „   All's Well that Ends Well.
101.   „   Antony and Cleopatra.
39.   „   As You Like It.
74.   „   Coriolanus.
97.   „   Cymbeline.
18.   „   Hamlet.
78.   „   Henry IV., Part I.
79.   „   „   Part II.
03.   „   Henry V.
12.   „   Henry VIII.
103.   „   Julius Cæsar.
104.   „   King Henry VI.—Part I.
105.   „   „   „   „ II.
106.   „   „   „   „ III.
48.   „   King John.
        „   King Lear.
71.   „   Love's Labour Lost.
8.   „   Macbeth.
93.   „   Measure for Measure.
55.   „   Merry Wives of Windsor.
         „   Much Ado about Nothing.
32.   „   Othello.
107.   „   Pericles.
3.   „   Richard II.
83.   „   Richard III.
44.   „   Romeo and Juliet.
68.   „   The Comedy of Errors.
14.   „   The Merchant of Venice.
89.   „   The Taming of the Shrew.
29.   „   The Tempest. [Verona.
91.   „   The Two Gentlemen of
102.   „ · Timon of Athens.
108.   „   Titus Andronicus.
106.   „   Troilus and Cressida.
26.   „   Twelfth Night.
66. Shelley—Prometheus Unbound.
75.   „   Banquet of Plato.
23. Sheridan's Plays—"The Rivals" and "The School for Scandal."
49. Socrates—Memorable Thoughts of.
30. Southey's Life of Nelson.
33. Steele and Addison's Sir Roger de Coverley.
80. Steele's Essays and Tales.
2. Sterne (L.)—A Sentimental Journey. Intro. L. F. AUSTIN.
76. Swift's Battle of the Books.
13. Tennyson's Poems—(Selection). Intro. A. T. QUILLER-COUCH.
11. Thackeray (W. M.)—The Four Georges. Intro. L. F. AUSTIN.
27. Walpole's (Horace) Letters (Selection). Intro. STUART J. REID.
45. Walton (Isaac)—The Complete Angler.
69. Wordsworth's Poems—(Selection).

"The volumes are neatly bound in cloth, clearly printed, and the price a mere sixpence. . . . There are many series of reprints of British Classics, but none more handy or more adequate than these excellent little volumes."—*Academy*.

CASSELL & COMPANY, LIMITED, *London ; Paris, New York, Toronto & Melbourne.*

JOSEPH ADDISON.

From the Portrait by Michael Dahl,
in the National Portrait Gallery.

Sir Roger de Coverley

and

The Spectator's Club

By

Richard Steele and Joseph Addison

Introduction by
HENRY MORLEY

CASSELL AND COMPANY, LIMITED
LONDON, PARIS, NEW YORK, TORONTO AND MELBOURNE

824
A1
4.4

INTRODUCTION

RICHARD STEELE and JOSEPH ADDISON were almost of the same age. They were both born in the year 1672—Steele, a lawyer's son, in Dublin, about the 12th of March (1671, old style); Addison in a Wiltshire parsonage on the following 1st of May. Steele had already lost both father and mother, and was very friendless, when he was sent to Charterhouse School as a boy on the foundation. There he first met Joseph Addison.

Addison came of a clerical family; his father, Lancelot, had been a poor clergyman. His grandfather had held a poor living in Westmoreland. His mother was a clergyman's daughter. An uncle became Bishop of Bristol when that see gave the title of Bishop with an income of £400 a year. Addison's father, however, was an able man, and had a friend in Joseph Williamson, afterwards Sir Joseph, and a Secretary of State, who gave him the living of Milston, in Wiltshire, worth £120 a year. On this he had married, and the firstborn of the marriage was gratefully named Joseph, after the patron who had made marriage possible. The same patron continued his good offices, and Lancelot Addison had become Dean of Lichfield when he sent his son Joseph to the Charterhouse.

Steele and Addison as schoolboys were alike in deep-seated religious feeling, and in the possession of that genius which has made their names still pleasant in our ears. They differed greatly in external accidents of character. Steele, with an Irish warmth of kindliness, was frank, social, forgetful of himself; Addison was reserved, shy, and, except in free intercourse with a few intimate friends, embarrassed by self-consciousness. These were mere differences of temperament that made each friend more delightful to the other ; the bond that held them friends for life came of their likeness in essentials.

At different dates, Addison and Steele went from school to different colleges at Oxford. Addison distinguished himself by scholarship, and excelled in writing Latin verse. He wrote also some pieces of English verse which Dryden printed in a volume of his " Miscellanies," and he sent, in 1695, to King William, through Lord Somers, a paper of verses on the capture of Namur. In 1697, Addison sent to the other chief among Whig statesmen, Charles Montagu, who was himself a wit and scholar, some Latin verses on the Peace of Ryswick. In 1699, Somers and Montagu drew Addison from preparation for the Church by offering him a travelling allowance of £300 a year to enable him to prepare himself for diplomatic service, and he had received a first appointment when the death of King William put an end to Addison's allowance, and to public occupation for the time. Addison, however, continued his travels, probably as companion or tutor to a young gentleman. Before his return to England his father died, and a little money came to him that enabled him to pay, with interest, his college debts. After Addison's return to England, Charles Montagu, remembering how the promising young Whig had been drawn aside, by promise of old Whigs, from the career for which he had been intended, took an early opportunity of helping Addison to recover his foothold on the path he had been asked to choose. At Montagu's suggestion, Godolphin invited Addison to write a poem on the Battle of Blenheim, gave him at once a small office of £200 a year as a Commissioner of Appeal in the Excise, and promised more. The poem written upon such invitation was " *The Campaign*," and upon its success Addison obtained further advancement.

Steele, at a time of public danger, had left college to enlist as a private in the Coldstream Guards, and had been made secretary to the colonel of the regiment, Lord Cates, who gave him an ensign's commission. As a guardsman, Steele had published, in 1701, his "Christian Hero : an Argument proving that no Principles but those of Religion are sufficient to make a Great Man." He had then written three lively comedies, free from the immorality and profaneness which then distinguished pieces written for the stage, and with earnestness at the heart of them all. Steele had rejoined his friend Addison when Addison returned to London from his travels, and even then, as he tells us, Steele had expressed to Addison a wish that they might some time or other publish a work, written by them both, which should bear the name of "The Monument" in memory of their friendship. "The Spectator" is that Monument.

Early in 1706 Addison was made Under-Secretary of State to Sir Charles Hedges. He remained in that office, at the end of the year, under Marlborough's son-in-law, the Earl of Sunderland, who became thenceforth Addison's especial patron. Addison wrote also in that year, for the unsuccessful opera of "Rosamond," a libretto, in which he found occasion for more celebration of the glory of the Duke of Marlborough. Steele, after short union with a wife who died soon after marriage, was married in 1707 to a friend of his first wife's. Swift was, in those days, among his friends. Defoe's "Review," started on the 19th of February, 1704, was a political journal that had a supplement dealing with minor morals in a wholesome and diverting way. Steele seems to have thought this notion worth fuller development, and on the 12th of April, 1709, he began, under the name of "The Tatler," a penny paper, which appeared three times a week until its close on the 2nd of January, 1711.

The design of "The Tatler" was wholly Steele's invention. Addison was going to Ireland as chief secretary to Lord Wharton when the paper was about to appear, and only guessed its authorship from a passage in one of its earliest numbers. Addison sent a paper or two from Ireland but complete success had been secured by Steele, and eighty numbers had appeared, when Addison returned to town, and was drawn by his friend into full collaboration in a form of writing that, for the first time, gave play to his best powers. Steele, in his generous way, claimed as his own chief praise that, by the invention of this form of periodical essay addressed to the main body of English readers, he had given Addison to the world. But for this, Addison's sensitive reserve would have restricted him to the accepted forms of work that then allowed little room for the exquisite humour and the play of refined thought that charmed, in his talk, the private friends with whom alone he was at ease. Steele dropped "The Tatler" only for the bold purpose of reproducing it, as a daily penny paper, under the name of "The Spectator." He had been encouraged by success, and was confident in power of producing a daily essay with his friend Addison's help. "The Tatler" ended in 1711, on the 2nd of January. The first number of "The Spectator" appeared on the 1st of March, the two friends being then a little under forty years of age.

When "The Tatler" began its course, Swift had just been amusing the town in the character of Bickerstaff, a genuine astrologer, with his Prediction of the Death of Partridge the Almanac Maker, and the letter in which he professed to describe to a Person of Quality the "Fulfilment of the Prediction." Steele, taking up the joke, took up with it the name of Bickerstaff, and he was then led to develop the Astrologer into the constant figure of his "Tatler" paper.

To provide a corresponding centre of life for the new series, he sketched the plan of the Spectator Club, which he and Addison, with occasional help from friends, proceeded to develop, as is here set forth,

H. M.

SIR ROGER DE COVERLEY

AND

THE SPECTATOR'S CLUB

OF CLUBS IN GENERAL

*—Tigris agit rabidâ cum tigride pacem
Perpetuam, sævis inter se convenit ursis.*

JUV., *Sat.* xv. 163.

Tiger with tiger, bear with bear you'll find
In leagues offensive and defensive joined.

TATE.

MAN is said to be a sociable animal, and as an instance of it we may observe that we take all occasions and pretences of forming ourselves into those little nocturnal assemblies which are commonly known by the name of clubs. When a set of men find themselves agree in any particular, though never so trivial, they establish themselves into a kind of fraternity, and meet once or twice a week upon the account of such a fantastic resemblance. I know a considerable market-town, in which there was a club of fat men, that

A*—33

did not come together, as you may well suppose, to
entertain one another with sprightliness and wit, but
to keep one another in countenance. The room where
the club met was something of the largest, and had
two entrances; the one by a door of a moderate size,
and the other by a pair of folding-doors. If a candi-
date for this corpulent club could make his entrance
through the first, he was looked upon as unqualified;
but if he stuck in the passage, and could not force his
way through it, the folding-doors were immediately
thrown open for his reception, and he was saluted as a
brother. I have heard that this club, though it con-
sisted but of fifteen persons, weighed above three ton.

In opposition to this society, there sprung up another
composed of scarecrows and skeletons, who, being very
meagre and envious, did all they could to thwart the
designs of their bulky brethren, whom they represented as men of dangerous principles; till at length
they worked them out of the favour of the people, and
consequently out of the magistracy. These factions
tore the corporation in pieces for several years, till at
length they came to this accommodation : that the two
bailiffs of the town should be annually chosen out of the
two clubs; by which means the principal magistrates
are at this day coupled like rabbits, one fat and one
lean.

Every one has heard of the club, or rather the

confederacy of the Kings. This grand alliance was formed a little after the return of King Charles the Second, and admitted into it men of all qualities and professions, provided they agreed in this surname of King, which, as they imagined, sufficiently declared the owners of it to be altogether untainted with republican and anti-monarchical principles.

A Christian name has likewise been often used as a badge of distinction, and made the occasion of a club. That of the Georges, which used to meet at the sign of the George on St. George's day, and swear, "before George," is still fresh in every one's memory.

There are at present, in several parts of this city, what they call street clubs, in which the chief inhabitants of the street converse together every night. I remember, upon my inquiring after lodgings in Ormond Street, the landlord, to recommend that quarter of the town, told me there was at that time a very good club in it; he also told me, upon further discourse with him, that two or three noisy country squires, who were settled there the year before, had considerably sunk the price of house-rent; and that the club, to prevent the like inconveniences for the future, had thoughts of taking every house that became vacant into their own hands, till they had found a tenant for it of a sociable nature and good conversation.

The Hum-Drum Club, of which I was formerly an

unworthy member, was made up of very honest gentlemen of peaceable dispositions, that used to sit together,
smoke their pipes, and say nothing till midnight. The
Mum Club, as I am informed, is an institution of the
same nature, and as great an enemy to noise.

After these two innocent societies, I cannot forbear
mentioning a very mischievous one, that was erected
in the reign of King Charles the Second : I mean
the Club of Duellists, in which none was to be
admitted that had not fought his man. The president of it was said to have killed half a dozen
in single combat; and as for the other members, they
took their seats according to the number of their slain.
There was likewise a side table for such as had only
drawn blood, and shown a laudable ambition of taking
the first opportunity to qualify themselves for the first
table. This club, consisting only of men of honour,
did not continue long, most of the members of it being
put to the sword, or hanged, a little after its institution.

Our modern celebrated clubs are founded upon eating and drinking, which are points wherein most men
agree, and in which the learned and the illiterate, the
dull and the airy, the philosopher and the buffoon, can
all of them bear a part. The Kit-cat itself is said to
have taken its original from a mutton pie. The Beef-
steak and October Clubs are neither of them adverse to

eating and drinking, if we may form a judgment of them from their respective titles.

When men are thus knit together by a love of society, not a spirit of faction, and do not meet to censure or annoy those that are absent, but to enjoy one another; when they are thus combined for their own improvement, or for the good of others, or at least to relax themselves from the business of the day by an innocent and cheerful conversation, there may be something very useful in these little institutions and establishments.

I cannot forbear concluding this paper with a scheme of laws that I met with upon a wall in a little alehouse. How I came thither I may inform my reader at a more convenient time. These laws were enacted by a knot of artisans and mechanics, who used to meet every night; and, as there is something in them which gives us a pretty picture of low life, I shall transcribe them word for word.

Rules to be observed in the TWO-PENNY CLUB, *erected in this place for the preservation of friendship and good neighbourhood.*

I. Every member at his first coming in shall lay down his two-pence.

II. Every member shall fill his pipe out of his own box.

III. If any member absents himself, he shall forfeit a penny for the use of the club, unless in case of sickness or imprisonment.

IV. If any member swears or curses, his neighbour may give him a kick upon the shins.

V. If any member tells stories in the club that are not true, he shall forfeit for every third lie a halfpenny.

VI. If any member strikes another wrongfully, he shall pay his club for him.

VII. If any member brings his wife into the club, he shall pay for whatever she drinks or smokes.

VIII. If any member's wife comes to fetch him home from the club, she shall speak to him without the door.

IX. If any member calls another a cuckold, he shall be turned out of the club.

X. None shall be admitted into the club that is of the same trade with any member of it.

XI. None of the club shall have his clothes or shoes made or mended, but by a brother member.

XII. No non-juror shall be capable of being a member.

The morality of this little club is guarded by such wholesome laws and penalties that I question not but my reader will be as well pleased with them as he would have been with the *Leges Convivales* of Ben

Jonson, the regulations of an old Roman club cited by
Lipsius, or the rules of a *Symposium* in an ancient
Greek author.

THE SPECTATOR

Non fumum ex fulgore, sed ex fumo dare lucem
Cogitat, ut speciosa dehinc miracula promat.

HOR., *Ars. Poet.* 143.

One with a flash begins, and ends in smoke ;
Another out of smoke brings glorious light.
And, without raising expectations high,
Surprises us with dazzling miracles.

ROSCOMMON.

I HAVE observed that a reader seldom peruses a book
with pleasure till he knows whether the writer of it
be a black or a fair man, of a mild or choleric disposition, married or a bachelor, with other particulars
of the like nature that conduce very much to the right
understanding of an author. To gratify this curiosity,
which is so natural to a reader, I design this paper
and my next as prefatory discourses to my following
writings, and shall give some account in them of the
several persons that are engaged in this work. As
the chief trouble of compiling, digesting, and correct-
ing will fall to my share, I must do myself the justice
to open the work with my own history.

I was born to a small hereditary estate, which, according to the tradition of the village where it lies, was bounded by the same hedges and ditches in William the Conqueror's time that it is at present, and has been delivered down from father to son, whole and entire, without the loss or acquisition of a single field or meadow, during the space of six hundred years. There runs a story in the family, that when my mother was gone with child of me about three months, she dreamt that she was brought to bed of a judge. Whether this might proceed from a law-suit which was then depending in the family, or my father's being a justice of the peace, I cannot determine; for I am not so vain as to think it presaged any dignity that I should arrive at in my future life, though that was the interpretation which the neighbourhood put upon it. The gravity of my behaviour at my very first appearance in the world, and all the time that I sucked, seemed to favour my mother s dream; for, as she has often told me, I threw away my rattle before I was two months old, and would not make use of my coral till they had taken away the bells from it.

As for the rest of my infancy, there being nothing in it remarkable, I shall pass it over in silence. I find that during my nonage I had the reputation of a very sullen youth, but was always a favourite of my schoolmaster, who used to say "that my parts were solid, and would wear well" I had not been long at the University before I distinguished myself by a most profound silence; for during the space of eight years, excepting in the public exercises of the college, I scarce uttered the quantity of a hundred words; and, indeed, do not remember that I ever spoke three sentences together in my whole life. Whilst I was in this learned body, I applied myself with so much diligence to my studies that there are very few celebrated books, either in the learned or the modern tongues, which I am not acquainted with.

Upon the death of my father, I was resolved to travel into foreign countries, and therefore left the University, with the character of an odd, unaccountable fellow, that had a great deal of learning, if I would but show it. An insatiable thirst after knowledge carried me into all the countries of Europe in which there was anything new or strange to be seen; nay, to such a degree was my curiosity raised that, having read the controversies of some great men concerning the antiquities of Egypt, I made a voyage to Grand Cairo on purpose to take the measure of a pyramid; and, as soon as I had set myself right in that particular, returned to my native country with great satisfaction.

I have passed my latter years in this city, where I

am frequently seen in most public places, though there are not above half a dozen of my select friends that know me; of whom my next paper shall give a more particular account. There is no place of general resort wherein I do not often make my appearance. Sometimes I am seen thrusting my head into a round of politicians at Will's, and listening with great attention to the narratives that are made in those little circular audiences. Sometimes I smoke a pipe at Child's; and, whilst I seem attentive to nothing but the postman, overhear the conversation of every table in the room. I appear on Sunday nights at St. James's coffeehouse, and sometimes join the little committee of politics in the inner room, as one who comes there to hear and improve. My face is likewise very well known at the Grecian, the Cocoa-tree, and in the theatres both of Drury Lane and the Haymarket. I have been taken for a merchant upon the Exchange for above these ten years, and sometimes pass for a Jew in the assembly of stock-jobbers at Jonathan's. In short, wherever I see a cluster of people, I always mix with them, though I never open my lips but in my own club.

Thus I live in the world rather as a spectator of mankind than as one of the species, by which means I have made myself a speculative statesman, soldier, merchant, and artisan, without ever meddling with any practical part in life. I am very well versed in the theory of a husband, or a father, and can discern the errors in the economy, business, and diversion of others, better than those who are engaged in them; as standers-by discover blots which are apt to escape those who are in the game. I never espoused any party with violence, and am resolved to observe an exact neutrality between the Whigs and Tories, unless I shall be forced to 'declare myself by the hostilities of either side. In short, I have acted in all the parts of my life as a looker on, which is the character I intend to preserve in this paper.

I have given the reader just so much of my history and character as to let him see I am not altogether unqualified for the business I have undertaken. As for other particulars in my life and adventures, I shall insert them in the following papers as I shall see occasion. In the meantime, when I consider how much I have seen, read, and heard, I begin to blame my own taciturnity; and since I have neither time nor inclination to communicate the fulness of my heart in speech, I am resolved to do it in writing, and to print myself out, if possible, before I die. I have been often told by my friends that it is a pity so many useful discoveries which I have made should be in the possession of a silent man. For this reason, therefore, I shall publish a sheetful of thoughts every morning

for the benefit of my contemporaries ; and if I can any
way contribute to the diversion or improvement of the
country in which I live, I shall leave it, when I am
summoned out of it, with the secret satisfaction of
thinking that I have not lived in vain.

There are three very material points which I have
not spoken to in this paper ; and which, for several
important reasons, I must keep to myself, at least for
some time : I mean an account of my name, my age,
and my lodgings. I must confess I would gratify my
reader in anything that is reasonable ; but, as for
these three particulars, though I am sensible they
might tend very much to the embellishment of my
paper, I cannot yet come to a resolution of communi-
cating them to the public. They would indeed draw
me out of that obscurity which I have enjoyed for
many years, and expose me in public places to several
salutes and civilities, which have been always very
disagreeable to me ; for the greatest pain I can suffer
is the being talked to, and being stared at. It is
for this reason, likewise, that I keep my complexion
and dress as very great secrets ; though it is not
impossible but I may make discoveries of both in the
progress of the work I have undertaken.

After having been thus particular upon myself, I
shall in to-morrow's paper give an account of those
gentlemen who are concerned with me in this work ;

for, as I have before intimated, a plan of it is laid and concerted, as all other matters of importance are, in a club. However, as my friends have engaged me to stand in the front, those who have a mind to correspond with me, may direct their letters to the Spectator, at Mr. Buckley's, in Little Britain. For I must further acquaint the reader that, though our club meets only on Tuesdays and Thursdays, we have appointed a committee to sit every night for the inspection of all such papers as may contribute to the advancement of the public weal.

THE SPECTATOR'S CLUB

—Ast alii sex
Et plures uno conclamant ore.—

Juv., *Sat.* vii. 166.

Six more at least join their consenting voice.

THE first of our society is a gentleman of Worcestershire, of ancient descent, a baronet; his name Sir Roger de Coverley. His great-grandfather was inventor of that famous country-dance which is called after him. All who know that shire are very well acquainted with the parts and merits of Sir Roger. He is a gentleman that is very singular in his

behaviour, but his singularities proceed from his good
sense, and are contradictions to the manners of the
world only as he thinks the world is in the wrong.
However, this humour creates him no enemies, for he
does nothing with sourness or obstinacy; and his
being unconfined to modes and forms makes him but
the readier and more capable to please and oblige all
who know him.   When he is in town, he lives in Soho
Square.   It is said he keeps himself a bachelor by
reason he was crossed in love by a perverse beautiful
widow of the next county to him.   Before this disappointment, Sir Roger was what you call a fine
gentleman, had often supped with my Lord Rochester
and Sir George Etherege, fought a duel upon his first
coming to town, and kicked bully Dawson in a public
coffee-house for calling him youngster.   But being
ill-used by the above-mentioned widow, he was very
serious for a year and a half; and though, his temper
being naturally jovial, he at last got over it, he grew
careless of himself, and never dressed afterwards.
He continues to wear a coat and doublet of the same
cut that were in fashion at the time of his repulse,
which, in his merry humours, he tells us, has been in
and out twelve times since he first wore it.   It
is said Sir Roger grew humble in his desires after
he had forgot this cruel beauty, insomuch that it
is reported he has frequently offended with beggars

and gipsies: but this is looked upon, by his friends, rather as matter of raillery than truth. He is now in his fifty-sixth year, cheerful, gay, and hearty; keeps a good house both in town and country; a great lover of mankind; but there is such a mirthful cast in his behaviour that he is rather beloved than esteemed.

His tenants grow rich, his servants look satisfied, all the young women profess love to him, and the young men are glad of his company. When he comes into a house, he calls the servants by their names, and talks all the way up-stairs to a visit. I must not omit that Sir Roger is a justice of the quorum: that he fills the chair at a Quarter Session with great abilities, and three months ago gained universal applause by explaining a passage in the Game Act.

The gentleman next in esteem and authority among us is another bachelor, who is a member of the Inner Temple, a man of great probity, wit, and understanding; but he has chosen his place of residence rather to obey the direction of an old humoursome father than in pursuit of his own inclinations. He was placed there to study the laws of the land, and is the most learned of any of the house in those of the stage. Aristotle and Longinus are much better understood by him than Littleton or Coke. The father sends up every post questions relating to marriage articles, leases, and tenures, in the neighbourhood; all which questions he agrees with an attorney to answer and take care of in the lump. He is studying the passions themselves, when he should be inquiring into the debates among men which arise from them. He knows the argument of each of the orations of Demosthenes and Tully, but not one case in the reports of our own courts. No one ever took him for a fool; but none, except his intimate friends, know he has a great deal of wit. This turn makes him at once both disinterested and agreeable. As few of his thoughts are drawn from business, they are most of them fit for conversation. His taste for books is a little too just for the age he lives in; he has read all, but approves of very few. His familiarity with the customs, manners, actions, and writings of the ancients, makes him a very delicate observer of what occurs to him in the present world. He is an excellent critic, and the time of the play is his hour of business : exactly at five he passes through New Inn, crosses through Russel Court, and takes a turn at Will's till the play begins; he has his shoes rubbed and his periwig powdered at the barber's as you go into the Rose. It is for the good of the audience when he is at the play, for the actors have an ambition to please him.

The person of next consideration is Sir Andrew Freeport, a merchant of great eminence in the city of London : a person of indefatigable industry, strong reason, and great experience. His notions of trade are noble and generous, and, as every rich man has usually some sly way of jesting, which would make no great figure were he not a rich man, he calls the sea the British Common. He is acquainted with commerce in all its parts; and will tell you it is a stupid and barbarous way to extend dominion by arms; for true power is to be got by arts and industry. He will often argue that, if this part of our trade were well cultivated, we should gain from one nation; and if another, from another. I have heard him prove that diligence makes more lasting acquisitions than valour, and that sloth has ruined more nations than the sword. He abounds in several frugal maxims, amongst which the greatest favourite is, "A penny saved is a penny got." A general trader of good sense is pleasanter company than a general scholar; and Sir Andrew having a natural unaffected eloquence, the perspicuity of his discourse gives the same pleasure that wit would in another man. He has made his fortunes himself: and says that England may be richer than other kingdoms by as plain methods as he himself is richer than other men; though at the same time I can say this of him, that there is not a point in the compass but blows home a ship in which he is an owner.

Next to Sir Andrew in the club-room sits Captain Sentry, a gentleman of great courage and understanding, but invincible modesty. He is one of those that deserve very well, but are very awkward at putting their talents within the observation of such as should take notice of them. He was some years a captain, and behaved himself with great gallantry in several engagements and at several sieges ; but having a small estate of his own, and being next heir to Sir Roger, he has quitted a way of life in which no man can rise suitably to his merit who is not something of a courtier as well as a soldier. I have heard him often lament that, in a profession where merit is placed in so conspicuous a view, impudence should get the better of modesty. When he has talked to this purpose, 1 never heard him make a sour expression, but frankly confess that he left the world because he was not fit for it. A strict honesty and an even regular behaviour are in themselves obstacles to him that must press through crowds, who endeavour at the same end with himself—the favour of a commander. He will, how-ever, in his way of talk, excuse generals for not dis-posing according to men's desert, or inquiring into it ; for, says he, that great man who has a mind to help me has as many to break through to come at me as I have to come at him; therefore, he will conclude, that the man who would make a figure, especially in a military way, must get over all false modesty, and assist his patron against the importunity of other pretenders, by a proper assurance in his own vindication. He says it is a civil cowardice to be backward in asserting what you ought to expect, as it is a military fear to be slow in attacking when it is your duty. With this candour does the gentleman speak of himself and others. The same frankness runs through all his conversation. The military part of his life has furnished him with many adventures, in the relation of which he is very agreeable to the company; for he is never overbearing, though accustomed to command men in the utmost degree below him; nor ever too obsequious, from a habit of obeying men highly above him.

But that our society may not appear a set of humourists, unacquainted with the gallantries and pleasures of the age, we have amongst us the gallant Will Honeycomb, a gentleman who, according to his years, should be in the decline of his life; but having ever been very careful of his person, and always had a very easy fortune, time has made but very little impression, either by wrinkles on his forehead or traces in his brain. His person is well turned, of a good height. He is very ready at that sort of discourse with which men usually entertain women. He is all his life dressed very well; and remembers habits as others do men. He can smile when one speaks to him, and laugh easily. He knows the history of every mode, and can inform you from which of the French

king's wenches our wives and daughters had this
manner of curling their hair, that way of placing their
hoods; whose frailty was covered by such a sort of
petticoat; and whose vanity to show her foot made
that part of the dress so short in such a year. In a
word, all his conversation and knowledge have been in
the female world. As other men of his age will take
notice to you what such a minister said upon such and
such an occasion, he will tell you when the Duke of
Monmouth danced at court, such a woman was then
smitten, another was taken with him at the head of his
troop in the park. In all these important relations, he
has ever about the same time received a kind glance,
or a blow of a fan, from some celebrated beauty, mother
of the present Lord Such-a-one. If you speak of a
young commoner that said a lively thing in the House,
he starts up, "He has good blood in his veins; Tom
Mirable begot him; the rogue cheated me in that
affair; that young fellow's mother used me more like
a dog than any woman I ever made advances to."
This way of talking of his very much enlivens the
conversation among us of a more sedate turn; and I
find there is not one of the company, but myself, who
rarely speak at all, but speaks of him as that sort of
man who is usually called a well-bred fine gentleman.
To conclude his character, where women are not concerned, he is an honest worthy man.

I cannot tell whether I am to account him whom I am next to speak of as one of our company; for he visits us but seldom, but when he does it adds to every man else a new enjoyment of himself. He is a clergyman, a very philosophic man, of general learning, great sanctity of life, and the most exact breeding. He has the misfortune to be of a very weak constitution, and, consequently, cannot accept of such cares and business as preferments in his function would oblige him to; he is, therefore, among divines what a chamber-counsellor is among lawyers. The probity of his mind, and the integrity of his life, create him followers, as being eloquent or loud advances others. He seldom introduces the subject he speaks upon; but we are so far gone in years that he observes, when he is among us, an earnestness to have him fall on some divine topic which he always treats with much authority, as one who has no interest in this world, as one who is hastening to the object of all his wishes, and conceives hope from his decays and infirmities. These are my ordinary companions.

SIR ROGER ON MEN OF PARTS

Credebant hoc grande nefas, et morte piandum,
Si juvenis vetulo non assurrexerat.

                                    JUV., *Sat.* xiii. 54.

'T was impious then, so much was age revered,
For youth to keep their seats when an old man appeared.

I KNOW no evil under the sun so great as the abuse of
the understanding; and yet there is no one vice more
common. It has diffused itself through both sexes,
and all qualities of mankind; and there is hardly that
person to be found who is not more concerned for the
reputation of wit and sense than honesty and virtue.
But this unhappy affectation of being wise rather than
honest, witty than good-natured, is the source of most
of the ill-habits of life. Such false impressions are
owing to the abandoned writings of men of wit, and
the awkward imitation of the rest of mankind.

For this reason, Sir Roger was saying last night
that he was of opinion none but men of fine parts
deserved to be hanged. The reflections of such men
are so delicate upon all occurrences which they are
concerned in that they should be exposed to more
than ordinary infamy and punishment for offending

against such quick admonitions as their own souls give them, and blunting the fine edge of their minds in such a manner that they are no more shocked at vice and folly than men of slower capacities. There is no greater monster in being than a very ill man of great parts. He lives like a man in a palsy, with one side of him dead. While perhaps he enjoys the satisfaction of luxury, of wealth, of ambition, he has lost the taste of good-will, of friendship, of innocence. Scarecrow, the beggar in Lincoln's Inn Fields, who disabled himself in his right leg, and asks alms all day to get himself a warm supper and a trull at night, is not half so despicable a wretch as such a man of sense. The beggar has no relish above sensations; he finds rest more agreeable than motion; and, while he has a warm fire, never reflects that he deserves to be whipped. Every man who terminates his satisfactions and enjoyments within the supply of his own necessities and passions is, says Sir Roger, in my eye, as poor a rogue as Scarecrow. "But," continued he, "for the loss of public and private virtue, we are beholden to your men of parts, forsooth; it is with them no matter what is done, so it is done with an air. But to me, who am so whimsical in a corrupt age as to act according to nature and reason, a selfish man, in the most shining circumstance and equipage, appears in the same condition with the fellow above-mentioned, but more contemptible, in proportion to what more he robs the public of and enjoys above him. I lay it down, therefore, for a rule that the whole man is to move together; that every action of any importance is to have a prospect of public good; and that the general tendency of our indifferent actions ought to be agreeable to the dictates of reason, of religion, of good-breeding: without this, a man, as I before have hinted, is hopping instead of walking; he is not in his entire and proper motion."

While the honest knight was thus bewildering himself in good starts, I looked intently upon him, which made him, I thought, collect his mind a little. "What I aim at," says he, "is to represent, that I am of opinion to polish our understandings and neglect our manners is of all things the most inexcusable. Reason should govern passion; but, instead of that, you see, it is often subservient to it; and, as unaccountable as one would think it, a wise man is not always a good man." This degeneracy is not only the guilt of particular persons, but also at some times of a whole people; and perhaps it may appear upon examination that the most polite ages are the least virtuous. This may be attributed to the folly of admitting wit and learning as merit in themselves, without considering the application of them. By this means it becomes a rule, not so much to regard what we do, as how we do it. But this false beauty will not pass upon men of honest minds and true taste. Sir Richard Blackmore says, with as much good sense as virtue, "It is a mighty dishonour and shame to employ excellent faculties and abundance of wit to humour and please men in their vices and follies. The great enemy of mankind, notwithstanding his wit and angelic faculties, is the most odious being in the whole creation." He goes on soon after to say, very generously, that he undertook the writing of his poem "to rescue the Muses out of the hands of ravishers; to restore them to their sweet and chaste. mansions; and to engage them in an employment suitable to their dignity." This certainly ought to be the purpose of every man who appears in public; and whoever does not proceed upon that foundation injures his country as fast as he succeeds in his studies. When modesty ceases to be the chief ornament of one sex, and integrity of the other, society is upon a wrong basis; and we shall be ever after without rules to guide our judgment in what is really becoming and ornamental. Nature and reason direct one thing; passion and humour another. To follow the dictates of the two latter is going into a road that is both endless and intricate; when we pursue the other, our passage is delightful, and what we aim at easily attainable.

I do not doubt but England is at present as polite a
nation as any in the world ; but any man who thinks
can easily see that the affectation of being gay and in
fashion has very near eaten up our good sense and our
religion. Is there anything so just as that mode and
gallantry should be built upon exerting ourselves in
what is proper and agreeable to the institutions of
justice and piety among us? And yet is there anything more common than that we run in perfect con-
tradiction to them? All which is supported by no
other pretension than that it is done with what we
call a good grace.

Nothing ought to be held laudable or becoming,
but what nature itself should prompt us to think so.
Respect to all kind of superiors is founded, methinks,
upon instinct; and yet what is so ridiculous as age?
I make this abrupt transition to the mention of this
vice more than any other, in order to introduce a little
story, which I think a pretty instance that the most
polite age is in danger of being the most vicious.

" It happened at Athens, during a public representa-
tion of some play exhibited in honour of the commonwealth, that an old gentleman came too late for a
place suitable to his age and quality. Many of the
young gentlemen who observed the difficulty and confusion he was in made signs to him that they would
accommodate him if he came where they sat. The

good man bustled through the crowd accordingly; but when he came to the seats to which he was invited, the jest was to sit close and expose him, as he stood, out of countenance, to the whole audience. The frolic went round all the Athenian benches. But on those occasions there were also particular places assigned for foreigners. When the good man skulked towards the boxes appointed for the Lacedæmonians, that honest people, more virtuous than polite, rose up all to a man, and with the greatest respect received him among them. The Athenians, being suddenly touched with a sense of the Spartan virtue and their own degeneracy, gave a thunder of applause; and the old man cried out, 'The Athenians understand what is good, but the Lacedæmonians practise it.' "

THE SPECTATOR IN LODGINGS

—*Veteres avias tibi de pulmone revello.*

PERS., *Sat.* v. 92.

I root th' old woman from thy trembling heart.

AT my coming to London, it was some time before I could settle myself in a house to my liking. I was forced to quit my first lodgings by reason of an officious landlady that would be asking me every morning how I had slept. I then fell into an honest family, and lived very happily for above a week ; when my landlord, who was a jolly, good-natured man, took it into his head that I wanted company, and therefore would frequently come into my chamber to keep me from being alone. This I bore for two or three days ; but telling me one day that he was afraid I was melancholy, I thought it was high time for me to be gone, and accordingly took new lodgings that very night. About a week after, I found my jolly landlord, who, as I said before, was an honest, hearty man, had put me into an advertisement in the *Daily Courant*, in the following words : " Whereas, a melancholy man left his lodgings on Thursday last in the afternoon, and was afterwards seen going towards Islington ; if any one can give notice of him to R. B., fishmonger in the Strand, he shall be very well rewarded for his pains." As I am the best man in the world to keep my own counsel, and my landlord the fishmonger not knowing my name, this accident of my life was never discovered to this very day.

I am now settled with a widow woman, who has a great many children, and complies with my humour in everything. I do not remember that we have exchanged a word together these five years ; my coffee comes into my chamber every morning without asking for it; if I want fire, I point to my chimney; if water, to my basin; upon which my landlady nods, as much as to say she takes my meaning, and immediately obeys my signals. She has likewise modelled her family so well that when her little boy offers to pull me by the coat, or prattle in my face, his eldest sister immediately calls him off, and bids him not to disturb the gentleman. At my first entering into the family, I was troubled with the civility of their rising up to me every time I came into the room; but my landlady observing that upon these occasions I always cried "Pish!" and went out again, has forbidden any such ceremony to be used in the house; so that at present I walk into the kitchen or parlour without being taken notice of or giving any interruption to the business or discourse of the family. The maid will ask her mistress, though I am by, whether the gentleman is ready to go to dinner, as the mistress, who is indeed an excellent housewife, scolds at the servants as heartily before my face as behind my back. In short, I move up and down the house, and enter into all companies, with the same liberty as a cat, or any other domestic animal, and am as little suspected of telling anything that I hear or see.

I remember last winter there were several young girls of the neighbourhood sitting about the fire with my landlady's daughters, and telling stories of spirits and

apparitions. Upon my opening the door the young
women broke off their discourse, but my landlady's
daughters telling them that it was nobody but the gentleman, for that is the name that I go by in the neighbourhood as well as in the family, they went on without minding me. I seated myself by the candle that stood on a
table at one end of the room, and, pretending to read
a book that I took out of my pocket, heard several
dreadful stories of ghosts as pale as ashes that had
stood at the feet of a bed, or walked over a churchyard by moonlight; and of others that had been con-
jured into the Red Sea, for disturbing people's rest
and drawing their curtains at midnight; with many
other old women's fables of the like nature. As one
spirit raised another, I observed that at the end of
every story, the whole company closed their ranks,
and crowded about the fire. I took notice in particular
of a little boy, who was so attentive to every story
that I am mistaken if he ventures to go to bed
by himself this twelvemonth. Indeed, they talked
so long that the imaginations of the whole assembly
were manifestly crazed, and I am sure will be the
worse for it as long as they live. I heard one of the
girls, that had looked upon me over her shoulder,
asking the company how long I had been in the room,
and whether I did not look paler than I used to do.
This put me under some apprehensions that I should

be forced to explain myself if I did not retire; for
which reason I took the candle into my hand, and
went up into my chamber, not without wondering at
this unaccountable weakness in reasonable creatures,
that they should love to astonish and terrify one
another. Were I a father, I should take a particulai
care to preserve my children from these little horrors
of imagination, which they are apt to contract when
they are young, and are not able to shake off when
they are in years. I have known a soldier that has
entered a breach, affrighted at his own shadow, and
look pale upon a little scratching at his door, who
the day before had marched up against a battery of
cannon. There are instances of persons who have
been terrified, even to distraction, at the figure of a
tree, or the shaking of a bulrush. The truth of it is, I
look upon a sound imagination as the greatest blessing
of life, next to a clear judgment and a good conscience.
In the meantime, since there are very few whose
minds are not more or less subject to these dreadful
thoughts and apprehensions, we ought to arm ourselves
against them by the dictates of reason and religion,
" to pull the old woman out of our hearts," as Persius
expresses it in the motto of my paper, and extinguish
those impertinent notions which we imbibe at a time
that we are not able to judge of their absurdity. Or,
if we believe, as many wise and good men have done,

that there are such phantoms and apparitions as those I have been speaking of, let us endeavour to establish to ourselves an interest in Him who holds the reins of the whole creation in His hand, and moderates them after such a manner, that it is impossible for one being to break loose upon another without His knowledge and permission.

For my own part, I am apt to join in the opinion with those who believe that all the regions of nature swarm with spirits, and that we have multitudes of spectators on all our actions, when we think ourselves most alone; but instead of terrifying myself with such a notion, I am wonderfully pleased to think that I am always engaged with such an innumerable society in searching out the wonders of the creation, and joining in the same *consort* of praise and adoration.

Milton has finely described this mixed communion of men and spirits in Paradise; and had doubtless his eye upon a verse in old Hesiod, which is almost word for word the same with his third line in the following passage:

> —Nor think, though men were none,
> That heaven would want spectators, God want praise:
> Millions of spiritual creatures walk the earth
> Unseen, both when we wake and when we sleep;
> All these with ceaseless praise His works behold

Both day and night.   How often from the steep
Of echoing hill or thicket have we heard
Celestial voices to the midnight air,
Sole, or responsive each to other's note,
Singing their great Creator ?   Oft in bands,
While they keep watch, or nightly rounding walk,
With heavenly touch of instrumental sounds,
· In full harmonic number joined, their songs
Divide the night, and lift our thoughts to heaven.

Parad. Lost., iv. 675.

PERSONAL APPEARANCE

—Tetrum ante omnia vultum.

JUV. x. 191.

—A visage rough,
Deformed, unfeatured.

SINCE our persons are not of our own making, when they are such as appear defective or uncomely, it is, methinks, an honest and laudable fortitude to dare to be ugly ; at least to keep ourselves from being abashed with a consciousness of imperfections which we cannot help, and in which there is no guilt.   I would not defend a haggard beau for passing away much time at a glass, and giving softnesses and languishing graces to
B*—33

deformity. All I intend is that we ought to be contented
with our counntenance and shape, so far as never to
give ourselves an uneasy reflectiou on that subject. It is
to the ordinary people, who are not accustomed to
make very proper remarks on any occasion, matter of
great jest if a man enters with a prominent pair of
shoulders into an assembly, or is distinguished by an
expansion of mouth, or obliqnity of aspect. It is
happy for a man that has any of these oddnesses about
him if he can be as merry upou himself as others are
apt to be upon that occasion. When he can possess himself with such a cheerfulness, women and children,
who were at first frighted at him, will afterwards
be as much pleased with him. As it is barbarous
in others to rally him for natural defects, it is extremely agreeable when he can jest upon himself for
them.

Madame Maintenon's first husband was a hero in this
kind, and has drawn many pleasantries from the irre-
gularity of his shape, which he describes as very much
resembling the letter Z. He diverts himself likewise
by representing to his reader the make of an engine
and pulley, with which he used to take off his hat.
When there happens to be anything ridiculous in a.
visage, and the owner of it thinks it an aspect of dignity, he must be of very great quality to be exempt
from raillery. The best expedient, therefore, is to be

pleasant upon himself.   Prince Harry and Falstaff, in
Shakespeare, have carried the ridicule upon fat and lean
as far as it will go.   Falstaff is humorously called
woolsack, bedpresser, and hill of flesh.   Harry a starve-
ling, an elf-skin, a sheath, a bow-case, and a tuck.   There
is, in several incidents of the conversation between
them, the jest still kept up upon the person.   Great
tenderness and sensibility in this point is one of the
greatest weaknesses of self-love.   For my own part,
I am a little unhappy in the mould of my face, which
is not quite so long as it is broad.   Whether this might
not partly arise from my opening my mouth much
seldomer than other people, and by consequence not so
much lengthening the fibres of my visage, I am not at
leisure to determine.   However it be, I have been often
put out of countenance by the shortness of my face,
and was formerly at great pains in concealing it by
wearing a periwig with a high foretop, and letting my
beard grow.   But now I have thoroughly got over this
delicacy, and could be contented it were much shorter,
provided it might qualify me for a member of the
merry club which the following letter gives me an
account of.   I have received it from Oxford; and, as it
abounds with the spirit of mirth and good-humour
which is natural to that place, I shall set it down word
for word as it came to me.

"MOST PROFOUND SIR,

"Having been very well entertained in the last of your speculations that I have yet seen, by your specimen upon clubs, which I therefore hope you will continue, I shall take the liberty to furnish you with a brief account of such a one as perhaps you have not seen in all your travels, unless it was your fortune to touch upon some of the woody parts of the African continent, in your voyage to or from Grand Cairo. There have arose in this University, long since you left us without saying anything, several of these inferior hebdomadal societies, as the Punning Club, the Witty Club, and, amongst the rest, the Handsome Club; as a burlesque upon which, a certain merry species that seem to have come into the world in masquerade, for some years last past have associated themselves together, and assumed the name of the Ugly Club. This ill-favoured fraternity consists of a president and twelve fellows; the choice of which is not confined by patent to any particular foundation, as St. John's men would have the world believe, and have therefore erected a separate society within themselves, but liberty is left to elect from any school in Great Britain, provided the candidates be within the rules of the club, as set forth in a table, entitled, The Act of Deformity, a clause or two of which I shall transmit to you.

"I. That no person whatsoever shall be admitted without a visible queerity in his aspect, or peculiar cast of countenance; of which the president and officers for the time being are to determine, and the president to have the casting voice.

"II. That a singular regard be had, upon examination, to the gibbosity of the gentlemen that offer themselves as founder's kinsmen; or to the obliquity of the figure, in what sort soever.

"III. That if the quantity of any man's nose be eminently miscalculated, whether as to length or breadth, he shall have a just pretence to be elected.

"Lastly, That if there shall be two or more competitors for the same vacancy, *cæteris paribus*, he that has the thickest skin to have the preference.

"Every fresh member, upon his first night, is to entertain the company with a dish of codfish, and a speech in praise of Æsop, whose portraiture they have in full proportion, or rather disproportion, over the chimney; and their design is, as soon as their funds are sufficient, to purchase the heads of Thersites, Duns Scotus, Scarron, Hudibras, and the old gentleman in Oldham, with all the celebrated ill faces of antiquity, as furniture for the club-room.

"As they have always been professed admirers of the other sex, so they unanimously declare that they will give all possible encouragement to such as will take the benefit of the statute, though none yet have appeared to do it.

" The worthy president, who is their utmost devoted champion, has lately shown me two copies of verses, composed by a gentleman of his society ; the first, a congratulatory ode, inscribed to Mrs. Touchwood, upon the loss of her two fore teeth ; the other a panegyric upon Mrs. Andiron's left shoulder. Mrs. Vizard, he says, since the small-pox, is grown tolerably ugly, and a top toast in the club ; but I never heard him so lavish of his fine things as upon old Nell Trot, who constantly officiates at their table ; her he even adores and extols as the very counterpart of Mother Shipton ; in short, Nell, says he, is one of the extraordinary works of nature ; but as for complexion, shape, and features, so valued by others, they are all mere outside and sym-metry, which is his aversion. Give me leave to add that the president is a facetious, pleasant gentleman, and never more so than when he has got, as he calls them, his dear mummers about him ; and he often protests it does him good to meet a fellow with a right genuine grimace in his air, which is so agreeable in the generality of the French nation ; and, as an instance of his sincerity in this particular, he gave me a sight of a list in his pocket-book of all of this class, who for these five years have fallen under his observation, with himself at the head of them, and in the rear, as one of a promising and improving aspect,

"Sir,

"Your obliged and humble servant,

"ALEXANDER CARBUNCLE.

"Oxford, March 12, 1710."

THE SPECTATOR AT HIS CLUB

—parcit

Cognatis maculis similis fera.—

JUV., *Sat.* xv. 159.

From spotted skins the leopard does refrain.

TATE.

THE club of which I am a member is very luckily composed of such persons as are engaged in different ways of life, and deputed as it were out of the most conspicuous classes of mankind. By this means I am furnished with the greatest variety of hints and materials, and know everything that passes in the different quarters and divisions, not only of this great city, but of the whole kingdom. My readers, too, have the satisfaction to find that there is no rank or degree

among them who have not their representative in this
club, and that there is always somebody present who
will take care of their respective interests, that nothing
may be written or published to the prejudice or in-
fringement of their just rights and privileges.

I last night sate very late in company with this
select body of friends, who entertained me with several
remarks which they and others had made upon these
my speculations, as also with the various success which
they had met with among their several ranks and
degrees of readers.   Will Honeycomb told me, in the
softest manner he could, that there were some ladies,
"but for your comfort," says Will, "they are not those
of the most wit," that were offended at the liberties I
had taken with the opera and the puppet-show ; that
some of them were likewise very much surprised that I
should think such serious points as the dress and
equipage of persons of quality proper subjects for
raillery.

He was going on, when Sir Andrew Freeport took
him up short, and told him that the papers he hinted at
had done great good in the city, and that all their
wives and daughters were the better for them ; and
further added that the whole city thought themselves
very much obliged to me for declaring my generous
intentions to scourge vice and folly as they appear in
a multitude, without condescending to be a publisher

of particular intrigues and cuckoldoms. "In short," says Sir Andrew, "if you avoid that foolish beaten road of falling upon aldermen and citizens, and employ your pen upon the vanity and luxury of courts, your paper must needs be of general use."

Upon this my friend the Templar told Sir Andrew that he wondered to hear a man of his sense talk after that manner; that the city had always been the province for satire; and that the wits of King Charles's time jested upon nothing else during his whole reign. He then showed, by the examples of Horace, Juvenal, Boileau, and the best writers of every age, that the follies of the stage and court had never been accounted too sacred for ridicule, how great soever the persons might be that patronised them. "But after all," says he, "I think your raillery has made too great an excursion in attacking several persons of the Inns of Court; and I do not believe you can show me any precedent for your behaviour in that particular."

My good friend Sir Roger de Coverley, who had said nothing all this while, began his speech with a "Pish!" and told us that he wondered to see so many men of sense so very serious upon fooleries. "Let our good friend," says he, "attack every one that deserves it; I would only advise you, Mr. Spectator," applying himself to me, "to take care how you meddle with country squires. They are the ornaments of the

English nation; men of good heads and sound bodies; and, let me tell you, some of them take it ill of you that you mention fox-hunters with so little respect."

Captain Sentry spoke very sparingly on this occasion. What he said was only to commend my prudence in not touching upon the army, and advised me to continue to act discreetly in that point.

By this time I found every subject of my speculations was taken away from me by one or other of the club; and began to think myself in the condition of the good man that had one wife who took a dislike to his grey hairs, and another to his black, till by their picking out what each of them had an aversion to, they left his head altogether bald and naked.

While I was thus musing with myself, my worthy friend the clergyman, who, very luckily for me, was at the club that night, undertook my cause. He told us that he wondered any order of persons should think themselves too considerable to be advised; that it was not quality, but innocence, which exempted men from reproof. That vice and folly ought to be attacked wherever they could be met with, and especially when they were placed in high and conspicuous stations of life. He further added that my paper would only serve to aggravate the pains of poverty, if it chiefly exposed those who are already depressed, and in some measure turned into ridicule by the meanness of their conditions and circumstances. He afterwards proceeded to take notice of the great use this paper might be of to the public by reprehending those vices which are too trivial for the chastisement of the law, and too fantastical for the cognisance of the pulpit. He then advised me to prosecute my undertaking with cheerfulness, and assured me that, whoever might be displeased with me, I should be approved by all those whose praises do honour to the persons on whom they are bestowed.

The whole club pays a particular deference to the discourse of this gentleman, and are drawn into what he says as much by the candid, ingenuous manner with which he delivers himself as by the strength of argument and force of reason which he makes use of. Will Honeycomb, immediately agreed that what he had said was right; and that, for his part, he would not insist upon the quarter which he had demanded for the ladies. Sir Andrew gave up the city with the same frankness. The Templar would not stand out, and was followed by Sir Roger and the Captain, who all agreed that I should be at liberty to carry the war into what quarter I pleased, provided I continued to combat with criminals in a body, and to assault the vice without hurting the person.

LEONORA

—Non illa colo calathisve Minervæ
Fæmineas assueta manus.—
VIRG., Æn. vii. 805.

Unbred to spinning, in the loom unskilled.
DRYDEN.

SOME months ago, my friend Sir Roger, being in the country, enclosed a letter to me, directed to a certain lady whom I shall here call by the name of Leonora, and, as it contained matters of consequence, desired me to deliver it to her with my own hand. Accordingly I waited upon her ladyship pretty early in the morning, and was desired by her woman to walk into her lady's library, till such time as she was in a readiness to receive me. The very sound of a lady's library gave me a great curiosity to see it; and as it was some time before the lady came to me, I had an opportunity of turning over a great many of her books, which were ranged together in a very beautiful order. At the end of the folios, which were finely bound and gilt, were great jars of china placed one above another in a very noble piece of architecture. The quartos were separated from the octavos by a pile of smaller vessels, which rose in a delightful pyramid. The octavos were bounded by tea-dishes of all shapes, colours, and sizes, which were so disposed on a wooden frame that they looked like one continued pillar indented with the finest strokes of sculpture, and stained with the greatest variety of dyes. That part of the library which was designed for the reception of plays and pamphlets and other loose papers was inclosed in a kind of square, consisting of one of the prettiest grotesque works that ever I saw, and made up of scaramouches, lions, monkeys, mandarines, trees, shells, and a thousand other odd figures in china-ware. In the midst of the room was a little Japan table, with a quire of gilt paper upon it, and on the paper a silver snuff-box made in the shape of a little book. I found there were several other counterfeit books upon the upper shelves, which were carved in wood, and served only to fill up the numbers, like fagots in the muster of a regiment. I was wonderfully pleased with such a mixed kind of furniture, as seemed very suitable to both the lady and the scholar, and did not know at first whether I should fancy myself in a grotto or in a library.

Upon my looking into the books, I found there were some few which the lady had bought for her own use, but that most of them had been got together, either because she had heard them praised, or because she had seen the authors of them.

Among several that I examined, I very well remember these that follow:

Ogleby's Virgil.

Dryden's Juvenal.

Cassandra.

Cleopatra.

Astræa.

Sir Isaac Newton's Works.

The Grand Cyrus; with a pin stuck in one of the
    middle leaves.

Pembroke's Arcadia.

Locke on Human Understanding; with a paper of
    patches in it.

A Spelling Book.

A Dictionary for the explanation of hard words.

Sherlock upon Death.

The Fifteen Comforts of Matrimony.

Sir William Temple's Essays.

Father Malebranche's Search after Truth, translated
    into English.

A book of Novels.

The Academy of Compliments.

Culpepper's Midwifery.

The Ladies' Calling.

Tales in Verse by Mr. D'Urfey: bound in red
    leather, gilt on the back, and doubled down in
    several places.

All the Classic Authors in Wood.

A set of Elzevirs by the same Hand.

Clelia; which opened of itself in the place that describes two lovers in a bower.

Baker's Chronicle.

Advice to a Daughter.

The New Atalantis, with a Key to it.

Mr. Steele's Christian Hero.

A Prayer-book; with a bottle of Hungary water by the side of it.

Dr. Sacheverell's Speech.

Fielding's Trial.

Seneca's Morals.

Taylor's Holy Living and Dying.

La Ferte's Instructions for Country Dances.

I was taking a catalogue in my pocket-book of these, and several other authors, when Leonora entered, and upon my presenting her with a letter from the knight, told me, with an unspeakable grace, that she hoped Sir Roger was in good health. I answered " Yes," for I hate long speeches, and, after a bow or two, retired.

Leonora was formerly a celebrated beauty, and is still a very lovely woman. She has been a widow for two or three years, and, being unfortunate in her first marriage, has taken a resolution never to venture upon a second. She has no children to take care of, and leaves the management of her estate to my good friend

Sir Roger. But as the mind naturally sinks into a kind of lethargy, and falls asleep, that is not agitated by some favourite pleasures and pursuits, Leonora has turned all the passions of her sex into a love of books and retirement. She converses chiefly with men, as she has often said herself, but it is only in their writings ; and admits of very few male visitants, except my friend Sir Roger, whom she hears with great pleasure and without scandal. As her reading has lain very much among romances, it has given her a very particular turn of thinking, and discovers itself even in her house, her gardens, and her furniture. Sir Roger has entertained me an hour together with a description of her country seat, which is situated in a kind of wilderness, about a hundred miles distant from London, and looks like a little enchanted palace. The rocks about her are shaped into artificial grottoes covered with woodbines and jessamines. The woods are cut into shady walks, twisted into bowers, and filled with cages of turtles. The springs are made to run among pebbles, and by that means taught to murmur very agreeably. They are likewise collected into a beautiful lake that is inhabited by a couple of swans, and empties itself by a little rivulet which runs through a green meadow, and is known in the family by the name of the Purling Stream. The knight likewise tells me that this lady preserves her game better than any of the gentlemen in the country, not, says Sir Roger, that she sets so great a value upon her partridges and pheasants as upon her larks and nightingales. For she says' that every bird which is killed in her ground will spoil a consort, and that she shall certainly miss him the next year.

When I think how oddly this lady is improved by learning, I look upon her with a mixture of admiration and pity. Amidst these innocent entertainments which she has formed to herself, how much more valuable does she appear than those of her sex who employ themselves in diversions that are less reasonable though more in fashion? What improvements would a woman have made, who is so susceptible of impressions from what she reads, had she been guided to such books as have a tendency to enlighten the understanding and rectify the passions, as well as to those which are of little more use than to divert the imagination?

PARTY ZEAL

Quem præstare potest mulier galeata pudorem,
Quæ fugit à sexu ?—

JUV., *Sat.* vi. 251.

What sense of shame in woman's breast can lie
Inured to arms, and her own sex to fly ?

DRYDEN.

THERE is one consideration which I would earnestly
recommend to all my female readers, and which, I
hope, will have some weight with them. In short, it
is this, that there is nothing so bad for the face as
party zeal. It gives an ill-natured cast to the eye, and
a disagreeable sourness to the look; besides that it
makes the lines too strong, and flushes them worse than
brandy. I have seen a woman's face break out in
heats, as she has been talking against a great lord,
whom she had never seen in her life; and indeed never
knew a party-woman that kept her beauty for a twelvemonth. I would therefore advise all my female readers,
as they value their complexions, to let alone all disputes
of this nature; though at the same time I would give
free liberty to all superannuated motherly partisans to
be as violent as they please, since there will be no

danger either of their spoiling their faces or of their gaining converts.

For my own part, I think a man makes an odious and despicable figure that is violent in a party; but a woman is too sincere to mitigate the fury of her principles with temper and discretion, and to act with that caution and reservedness which are requisite in our sex. When this unnatural zeal gets into them, it throws them into ten thousand heats· and extravagancies; their generous souls set no bounds to their love or to their hatred, and whether a Whig or Tory, a lapdog or gallant, an opera or a puppet-show, be the object of it, the passion, while it reigns, engrosses the whole woman.

I remember when Dr. Titus Oates was in all his glory, I accompanied my friend Will Honeycomb in a visit to a lady of his acquaintance. We were no sooner sat down, but, upon casting my eyes about the room, I found in almost every corner of it a print that represented the doctor in all magnitudes and dimensions. A little after, as the lady was discoursing with my friend, and held her snuff-box in her hand, who should I see in the lid of it but the doctor. It was not long after this when she had occasion for her handkerchief, which, upon the first opening, discovered among the plaits of it the figure of the doctor. Upon this my friend Will, who loves raillery, told her that if he was

in Mr. Truelove's place, for that was the name of her
husband, he should be made as uneasy by a handkerchief as ever Othello was. " I am afraid," said she,
" Mr. Honeycomb, you are a Tory : tell me truly, are
you a friend to the doctor or not ?" Will, instead of
making her a reply, smiled in her face, for indeed she
was very pretty, and told her that one of her patches
was dropping off. She immediately adjusted it, and
looking a little seriously, " Well," says she, " I will
be hanged if you and your silent friend there are not
against the doctor in your hearts; I suspected as much
by his saying nothing." Upon this she took her fan
into her hand, and upon the opening of it, again dis-
played to us the figure of the doctor, who was placed
with great gravity among the sticks of it. In a word,
I found that the doctor had taken possession of her
thoughts, her discourse, and most of her furniture;
but finding myself pressed too close by her question, I
winked upon my friend to take his leave, which he
did accordingly.

WILL HONEYCOMB'S ABSENCE OF MIND

Non convivere licet nec urbe totâ
Quisquam est tam propè, tam proculque nobis.

MART., *Ep.* i. 87.

What correspondence can I hold with you,
Who are so near, and yet so distant too?

MY friend Will Honeycomb is one of those sort of men who are very often absent in conversation, and what the French call *à reveur* and *a distrait*. A little before our club-time last night, we were walking together in Somerset Garden, where Will had picked up a small pebble of so odd a make that he said he would present it to a friend of his, an eminent virtuoso. After we had walked some time, I made a full stop with my face towards the west, which Will knowing to be my usual method of asking what's o'clock, in an afternoon, immediately pulled out his watch, and told me we had seven minutes good. We took a turn or two more, when, to my great surprise, I saw him squir away his watch a considerable way into the Thames, and, with great sedateness in his looks, put up the pebble, he had before found, in his fob. As I have naturally an aversion to much speaking, and do not love to be the messenger of ill news, especially when it comes too late to be useful, I left him to be convinced of his mistake in due time, and continued my walk, reflecting on these little absences and distractions in mankind, and resolving to make them a subject of a future speculation.

I was the more confirmed in my design when I considered that they were very often blemishes in the characters of men of excellent sense; and helped to keep up the reputation of that Latin proverb, which Mr. Dryden has translated in the following lines:

> Great wit to madness sure is near allied,
> And thin partitions do their bounds divide.

My reader does, I hope, perceive that I distinguish a man who is absent because he thinks of something else from one who is absent because he thinks of nothing at all. The latter is too innocent a creature to be taken notice of; but the distractions of the former may, I believe, be generally accounted for from one of these reasons:

Either their minds are wholly fixed on some particular science, which is often the case of mathematicians and other learned men; or are wholly taken up with some violent passion, such as anger, fear, or love, which ties the mind to some distant object; or, lastly, these distractions proceed from a certain vivacity and

fickleness in a man's temper, which, while it raises up
infinite numbers of ideas in the mind, is continually
pushing it on, without allowing it to rest on any particular image. Nothing, therefore, is more unnatural
than the thoughts and conceptions of such a man,
which are seldom occasioned either by the company he
is in or any of those objects which are placed before
him. [While you fancy he is admiring a beautiful
woman, it is an even wager that he is solving a propo-
sition in Euclid;] and while you may imagine he is
reading the *Paris Gazette*, it is far from being impossible
that he is pulling down and rebuilding the front of his
country house.

At the same time that I am endeavouring to expose
this weakness in others, I shall readily confess that I
once laboured under the same infirmity myself. The
method I took to conquer it was a firm resolution to
learn something from whatever I was obliged to see or
hear. There is a way of thinking, if a man can attain
to it, by which he may strike somewhat out of anything.
I can at present observe those starts of good sense, and
struggles of unimproved reason in the conversation of a
clown, with as much satisfaction as the most shining
periods of the most finished orator; and can make a
shift to command my attention at a puppet-show or
an opera as well as at *Hamlet* or *Othello*. I always
make one of the company I am in; for though I say

little myself, my attention to others, and those nods of approbation which I never bestow unmerited, sufficiently show that I am among them. Whereas, Will Honeycomb, though a fellow of good sense, is every day doing and saying a hundred things, which he afterwards confesses, with a well-bred frankness, were somewhat *mal a propos*, and undesigned.

I chanced the other day to go into a coffee-house, where Will was standing in the midst of several auditors, whom he had gathered round him, and was giving them an account of the person and character of Moll Hinton. My appearance before him just put him in mind of me, without making him reflect that I was actually present. So that keeping his eyes full upon me, to the great surprise of his audience, he broke off his first harangue, and proceeded thus :—" Why, now, there's my friend," mentioning me by name, "he is a fellow that thinks a great deal, but never opens his mouth ; I warrant you he is now thrusting his short face into some coffee-house about 'Change. I was his bail in the time of the Popish plot, when he was taken up for a Jesuit." If he had looked on me a little longer, he had certainly described me so particularly, without ever considering what led him into it, that the whole company must necessarily have found me out ; for which reason, remembering the old proverb, " Out of sight out of mind," I left the room ; and, upon meeting him an hour afterwards was asked by him, with a great deal of good humour, in what part of the world I lived, that he had not seen me these three days.

Monsieur Bruyere has given us the character of an absent man with a great deal of humour, which he has pushed to an agreeable extravagance ; with the heads of it I shall conclude my present paper.

"Menalcas," says that excellent author, "comes down in a morning, opens his door to go out, but shuts it again, because he perceives that he has his night-cap on ; and, examining himself further, finds that he is but half shaved, that he has stuck his sword on his right side, that his stockings are about his heels, and that his shirt is over his breeches. When he is dressed, he goes to court, comes into the drawing-room, and walking bolt-upright under a branch of candlesticks, his wig is caught up by one of them, and hangs dangling in the air. All the courtiers fall a laughing, but Menalcas laughs louder than any of them, and looks about for the person that is the jest of the company. Coming down to the court gate he finds a coach, which, taking for his own, he whips into it, and the coachman drives off, not doubting but he carries his master. As soon as he stops, Menalcas throws himself out of the coach, crosses the court, ascends the staircase, and runs through all the chambers with the greatest familiarity; reposes himself on a couch, and fancies himself at

c—33

home.   The master of the house at last comes in;
Menalcas rises to receive him, and desires him to sit
down; he talks, muses, and then talks again.   The
gentleman of the house is tired and amazed; Menalcas
is no less so, but is every moment in hopes that his impertinent guest will at last end his tedious visit.   Night
comes on, when Menalcas is hardly undeceived.

" When he is playing at backgammon, he calls for a
full glass of wine and water; it is his turn to throw;
he has the box in one hand, and his glass in the other;
and being extremely dry, and unwilling to lose time, he
swallows down both the dice, and at the same time
throws his wine into the tables.   He writes a letter,
and flings the sand into the ink-bottle; he writes a
second, and mistakes the superscription.   A nobleman
receives one of them, and, upon opening it, reads as
follows : ' I would have you, honest Jack, immediately
upon the receipt of this, take in hay enough to serve me
the winter.'   His farmer receives the other, and is amazed
to see in it, ' My lord, I received your grace's commands
with an entire submission to—.'   If he is at an entertainment, you may see the pieces of bread continually
multiplying round his plate.   It is true the rest of the
company want it, as well as their knives and forks,
which Menalcas does not let them keep long.   Sometimes in a morning he puts his whole family in a hurry,
and at last goes out without being able to stay for his

coach or dinner, and for that day you may see him in every part of the town, except the very place where he had appointed to be upon a business of importance. You would often take him for everything that he is not ; for a fellow quite stupid, for he hears nothing ; for a fool, for he talks to himself, and has a hundred grimaces and motions with his head, which are altogether involuntary ; for a proud man, for he looks full upon you, and takes no notice of your saluting him. The truth of it is, his eyes are open, but he makes no use of them, and neither sees you, nor any man, nor anything else. He came once from his country house, and his own footmen undertook to rob him, and succeeded. They held a flambeau to his throat, and bid him deliver his purse ; he did so, and coming home told his friends he had been robbed ; they desired to know the particulars, 'Ask my servants,' says Menalcas, 'for they were with me.'"

SIR ANDREW FREEPORT AND JACK TRUEPENNY

—Caput dominâ venale sub hastâ.

JUV., *Sat.* iii. 33.

His fortunes ruined, and himself a slave.

OUR gentry are, generally speaking, in debt; and
many families have put it into a kind of method of
being so from generation to generation. The father
mortgages when his son is very young; and the boy
is to marry, as soon as he is at age, to redeem it and
find portions for his sisters. This, forsooth, is no
great inconvenience to him; for he may wench, keep
a public table, or feed dogs, like a worthy English
gentleman, till he has outrun half his estate, and leave
the same encumbrance upon his firstborn, and so on;
till one man of more vigour than ordinary goes quite
through the estate: or some man of sense comes into
it, and scorns to have an estate in partnership, that is
to say, liable to the demand or insult of any man living.
There is my friend Sir Andrew, though for many
years a great and general trader, was never the defendant in a law suit; in all the perplexity of business,
and the iniquity of mankind at present, no one had any

colour for the least complaint against his dealings with him. This is certainly as uncommon, and in its proportion as laudable, in a citizen as it is in a general never to have suffered a disadvantage in fight. How different from this gentleman is Jack Truepenny, who has been an old acquaintance of Sir Andrew and myself from boys, but could never learn our caution. Jack has a whorish unresisting good-nature, which makes him incapable of having a property in anything. His fortune, his reputation, his time, and his capacity are at any man's service that comes first. When he was at school, he was whipped thrice a week for faults he took upon him to excuse others; since he came into the business of the world, he has been arrested twice or thrice a year for debts he had nothing to do with, but as surety for others; and I remember, when a friend of his had suffered in the vice of the town, all the physic his friend took was conveyed to him by Jack, and inscribed, "a bolus or an electuary for Mr. Truepenny." Jack had a good estate left him, which came to nothing, because he believed all who pretended to demands upon it. This easiness and credulity destroy all the other merit he has; and he has all his life been a sacrifice to others, without ever receiving thanks, or doing one good action.

I will end this discourse with a speech which I heard Jack make to one of his creditors, of whom he deserved gentler usage, after lying a whole night in custody at his suit:

"Sir, your ingratitude for the many kindnesses I have done you shall not make me unthankful for the good you have done me, in letting me see there is such a man as you in the world. I am obliged to you for the diffidence I shall have all the rest of my life. I shall hereafter trust no man so far as to be in his debt."

INSINCERE CIVILITIES

—*Sibi quivis*
Speret idem, sudet multùm, frustraque laboret
A usus idem.   HOR., *Ars. Poet.* 240.

Such all might hope to imitate with ease ;
Yet while they strive the same success to gain,
Should find their labour and their hopes are vain.
                                        FRANCIS.

MY friend the divine having been used with words of complaisance, which he thinks could be properly applied to no one living, and I think could be only spoken of him, and that in his absence, was so extremely offended with the excessive way of speaking civilities among us that he made a discourse against it at the club, which he concluded with this remark, " that he had not heard one compliment made in our society since its commencement." Every one was pleased with his conclusion ; and, as each knew his good-will to the rest, he was convinced that the many professions of kindness and service, which we ordinarily meet with, are not natural where the heart is well inclined; but are a prostitution of speech, seldom intended to mean any part of what they express, never to mean all they express. Our reverend friend, upon this topic, pointed to us two or three paragraphs on this subject in the first sermon of the first volume of the late archbishop's posthumous works. I do not know that I ever read anything that pleased me more ; and as it is the praise of Longinus that he speaks of the sublime in a style suitable to it, so one may say of this author upon sincerity, that he abhors any pomp of rhetoric on this occasion, and treats it with a more than ordinary simplicity, at once to be a preacher and an example. With what command of himself does he lay before us, in the language and temper of his profession, a fault which, by the least liberty and warmth of expression, would be the most lively wit and satire. But his heart was better disposed, and the good man chastised the great wit in such a manner that he was able to speak as follows :

" Amongst too many other instances of the great

corruption and degeneracy of the age wherein we live, the great and general want of sincerity in conversation is none of the least. The world is grown so full of dissimulation and compliment that men's words are hardly any signification of their thoughts ; and if any man measure his words by his heart, and speak as he thinks, and do not express more kindness to every man than men usually have for any man, he can hardly escape the censure of want of breeding. The old English plainness and sincerity, that generous integrity of nature and honesty of disposition which always argues true greatness of mind, and is usually accompanied with undaunted courage and resolution, is in a great measure lost amongst us. There hath been a long endeavour to transform us into foreign manners and fashions, and to bring us to a servile imitation of none of the best of our neighbours in some of the worst of their qualities. The dialect of conversation is now-a-days so swelled with vanity and compliment, and so surfeited, as I may say, of expressions of kindness and respect, that if a man that lived an age or two ago should return into the world again, he would really want a dictionary to help him to understand his own language, and to know the true intrinsic value of the phrase in fashion, and would hardly at first believe at what a low rate the highest strains and expressions of kindness imaginable do commonly pass in current payment; and when he should come to understand it, it would be a great while before he could bring himself with a good countenance and a good conscience to converse with men upon equal terms, and in their own way.

"And in truth it is hard to say whether it should more provoke our contempt or our pity to hear what solemn expressions of respect and kindness will pass between men, almost upon no occasion; how great honour and esteem they will declare for one whom perhaps they never saw before, and how entirely they are all on the sudden devoted to his service and interest, for no reason; how infinitely and eternally obliged to him, for no benefit; and how extremely they will be concerned for him, yea, and afflicted too, for no cause. I know it is said, in justification of this hollow kind of conversation, that there is no harm, no real deceit, in compliment, but the matter is well enough, so long as we understand one another; *et verba valent ut nummi*, ' words are like money;' and when the current value of them is generally understood, no man is cheated by them. This is something, if such words were any-thing, but, being brought into the account, they are mere cyphers. However, it is still a just matter of complaint that sincerity and plainness are out of fashion, and that our language is running into a lie; that men have almost quite perverted the use of speech,

c*—33

and made words to signify nothing; that the greatest part of the conversation of mankind is little else but driving a trade of dissimulation; insomuch that it would make a man heartily sick and weary of the world to see the little sincerity that is in use and practice among men."

When the vice is placed in this contemptible light, he argues unanswerably against it in words and thoughts so natural that any man who reads them would imagine he himself could have been author of them.

"If the show of anything be good for anything, I am sure sincerity is better; for why does any man dissemble, or seem to be that which he is not, but because he thinks it good to have such a quality as he pretends to? For to counterfeit and dissemble is to put on the appearance of some real excellency. Now, the best way in the world to seem to be anything is really to be what he would seem to be. Besides that, it is many times as troublesome to make good the pretence of a good quality as to have it; and if a man have it not, it is ten to one but he is discovered to want it; and then all his pains and labour to seem to have it are lost."

In another part of the same discourse he goes on to show that all artifice must naturally tend to the disappointment of him that practises it.

" Whatsoever convenience may be thought to be in falsehood and dissimulation, it is soon over ; but the inconvenience of it is perpetual, because it brings a man under an everlasting jealousy and suspicion, so that he is not believed when he speaks truth, nor trusted when perhaps he means honestly. When a man hath once forfeited the reputation of his integrity he is set fast, and nothing will then serve his turn. neither truth nor falsehood."

WILL HONEYCOMB'S PEDANTRY

—Id arbitror
Adprimè in vitâ esse utile, NE QUID NIMIS.
TER., *Andr.*, Act 1, Scene 1, 33.

I take it to be a principal rule of life, not to be too much addicted to any one thing.

Too much of anything is good for nothing.

Eng. Prov.

MY friend Will Honeycomb values himself very much upon what he calls the knowledge of mankind, which has cost him many disasters in his youth ; for Will reckons every misfortune that he has met with among the women, and every rencounter among the men, as

parts of his education; and fancies he should never
have been the man he is had not he broke windows,
knocked down constables, disturbed honest people with
his midnight serenades, and beat up a lewd woman's
quarters, when he was a young fellow. The engaging
in adventures of this nature Will calls the studying of
mankind; and terms this knowledge of the town the
knowledge of the world. Will ingenuously confesses
that for half his life his head ached every morning with
reading of men overnight; and at present comforts
himself under certain pains which he endures from time
to time, that without them he could not have been acquainted with the gallantries of the age. This Will
looks upon as the learning of a gentleman, and regards
all other kinds of science as the accomplishments of one
whom he calls a scholar, a bookish man, or a philosopher.

For these reasons Will shines in mixed company,
where he has the discretion not to go out of his depth,
and has often a certain way of making his real ignorance appear a seeming one. Our club, however, has
frequently caught him tripping, at which times they
never spare him. For as Will often insults us with
the knowledge of the town, we sometimes take our revenge upon him by our knowledge of books.

He was last week producing two or three letters
which he writ in his youth to a coquette lady. The
raillery of them was natural, and well enough for a

mere man of the town, but, very unluckily, several of the words were wrong spelt. Will laughed this off at first as well as he could; but, finding himself pushed on all sides, and especially by the Templar, he told us, with a little passion, that he never liked pedantry in spelling, and that he spelt like a gentleman, and not like a scholar. Upon this Will had recourse to his old topic of showing the narrow-spiritedness, the pride, and ignorance of pedants; which he carried so far that, upon my retiring to my lodgings, I could not forbear throwing together such reflections as occurred to me upon that subject.

A man who has been brought up among books, and is able to talk of nothing else, is a very indifferent companion, and what we call a pedant. But methinks we should enlarge the title, and give it every one that does not know how to think out of his profession and particular way of life.

What is a greater pedant than a mere man of the town? Bar him the play-houses, a catalogue of the reigning beauties, and an account of a few fashionable distempers that have befallen him, and you strike him dumb. How many a pretty gentleman's knowledge lies all within the verge of the Court? He will tell you the names of the principal favourites, repeat the shrewd sayings of a man of quality, whisper an intrigue that is not yet blown upon by common fame ; or, if the sphere of his observations is a little larger than ordinary, will perhaps enter into all the incidents, turns, and revolutions in a game of *ombre*. When he has gone thus far, he has shown you the whole circle of his accomplishments, his parts are drained, and he is disabled from any further conversation. What are these but rank pedants? and yet these are the men who value themselves most on their exemption from the pedantry of colleges.

I might here mention the military pedant who always talks in a camp, and is storming towns, making lodgments, and fighting battles from one end of the year to the other. Everything he speaks smells of gunpowder; if you take away his artillery from him, he has not a word to say for himself. I might likewise mention the law pedant, that is perpetually putting cases, repeating the transactions of Westminster Hall, wrangling with you upon the most indifferent circumstances of life, and not to be convinced of the distance of a place, or of the most trivial point in conversation but by dint of argument. The state pedant is wrapt up in news, and lost in politics. If you mention either of the kings of Spain or Poland, he talks very notably; but if you go out of the *Gazette*, you drop him. In short, a mere courtier, a mere soldier, a mere scholar, a mere anything, is an insipid pedantic character, and equally ridiculous.

Of all the species of pedants, which I have mentioned, the book pedant is much the most supportable; he has at least an exercised understanding, and a head which is full, though confused, so that a man who converses with him may often receive from him hints of things that are worth knowing, and what he may possibly turn to his own advantage, though they are of little use to the owner. The worst kind of pedants among learned men are such as are naturally endued with a very small share of common-sense, and have read a great number of books without taste or distinction.

The truth of it is, learning, like travelling, and all other methods of improvement, as it finishes good sense, so it makes a silly man ten thousand times more insufferable, by supplying variety of matter to his impertinence, and giving him an opportunity of abounding in absurdities.

Shallow pedants cry up one another much more than men of solid and useful learning. To read the titles they give an editor, or collator of a manuscript, you would take him for the glory of the commonwealth of letters, and the wonder of his age, when perhaps upon examination you find that he has only rectified a Greek particle, or laid out a whole sentence in proper commas.

They are obliged, indeed. to be thus lavish of their

praises that they may keep one another in countenance; and it is no wonder if a great deal of knowledge, which is not capable of making a man wise, has a natural tendency to make him vain and arrogant.

SIR ROGER DE COVERLEY AT HOME

—Hinc tibi copia
Manabit ad plenum, benigno
Ruris honorum opulenta cornu.

HOR., *Od.* i. 17, 14.

Here plenty's liberal horn shall pour
Of fruits for thee a copious shower,
Rich honours of the quiet plain.

HAVING often received an invitation from my friend Sir Roger de Coverley to pass away a month with him in the country, I last week accompanied him thither, and am settled with him for some time at his country house, where I intend to form several of my ensuing speculations. Sir Roger, who is very well acquainted with my humour, lets me rise and go to bed when I please, dine at his own table or in my chamber as I think fit, sit still and say nothing without bidding me be merry. When the gentlemen of the country come to see him, he only shows me at a distance. As I have been walking in his fields I have observed them stealing a sight of me over a hedge, and have heard the knight desiring them not to let me see them, for that I hated to be stared at.

I am the more at ease in Sir Roger's family, because it consists of sober and staid persons; for as the knight is the best master in the world, he seldom changes his servants; and as he is beloved by all about him, his servants never care for leaving him; by this means his domestics are all in years, and grown old with their master. You would take his valet de chambre for his brother, his butler is grey-headed, his groom is one of the gravest men that I have ever seen, and his coach-man has the looks of a privy-counsellor. You see the goodness of the master even in the old house-dog, and in a grey pad that is kept in the stable with great care and tenderness out of regard to his past services, though he has been useless for several years.

I could not but observe with a great deal of pleasure the joy that appeared in the countenances of these ancient domestics upon my friend's arrival at his country seat. Some of them could not refrain from tears at the sight of their old master; every one of them pressed forward to do something for him, and seemed discouraged if they were not employed. At the same time the good old knight, with a mixture of

the father and the master of the family, tempered the
inquiries after his own affairs with several kind questions relating to themselves.   This humanity and good-
nature engages everybody to him, so that when he is
pleasant upon any of them, all his family are in good
humour, and none so much as the person whom he
diverts himself with : on the contrary, if he coughs,
or betrays any infirmity of old age, it is easy for a
stander-by to observe a secret concern in the looks of
all his servants.

My worthy friend has put me under the particular
care of his butler, who is a very prudent man, and, as
well as the rest of his fellow-servants, wonderfully desirous of pleasing me, because they have often heard
their master talk of me as of his particular friend.

My chief companion, when Sir Roger is diverting
himself in the woods or the fields, is a very venerable
man who is ever with Sir Roger, and has lived at his
house in the nature of a chaplain above thirty years.
This gentleman is a person of good sense and some
learning, of a very regular life and obliging conversation : he heartily loves Sir Roger, and knows that he
is very much in the old knight's esteem, so that he
lives in the family rather as a relation than a de-
pendent.

I have observed in several of my papers that my
friend Sir Roger, amidst all his good qualities, is

something of a humorist; and that his virtues, as
well as imperfections, are, as it were, tinged by a
certain extravagance, which makes them particularly
his, and distinguishes them from those of other men.
This cast of mind, as it is generally very innocent in
itself, so it renders his conversation highly agreeable,
and more delightful than the same degree of sense and
virtue would appear in their common and ordinary
colours. As I was walking with him last night, he
asked me how I liked the good man whom I have just
now mentioned; and without staying for my answer
told me that he was afraid of being insulted with
Latin and Greek at his own table; for which reason he
desired a particular friend of his at the University to
find him out a clergyman rather of plain sense than
much learning, of a good aspect, a clear voice, a sociable
temper, and, if possible, a man that understood a little
of backgammon. "My friend," says Sir Roger,
"found me out this gentleman, who, besides the endow-
ments required of him, is, they tell me, a good scholar,
though he does not show it. I have given him the parsonage of the parish; and, because I know his value,
have settled upon him a good annuity for life. If he
outlives me, he shall find that he was higher in my
esteem than perhaps he thinks he is. He has now
been with me thirty years; and, though he does not
know I have taken notice of it, has never in all that

time asked anything of me for himself, though he is
every day soliciting me for something in behalf of one
or other of my tenants, his parishioners. There has
not been a law-suit in the parish since he has lived
among them; if any dispute arises, they apply themselves to him for the decision; if they do not acquiesce
in his judgment, which I think never happened above
once or twice at most, they appeal to me. At his first
settling with me I made him a present of all the good
sermons which have been printed in English, and only
begged of him that every Sunday he would pronounce
one of them in the pulpit. Accordingly he has
digested them into such a series that they follow one
another naturally, and make a continued system of
practical divinity."

As Sir Roger was going on in his story, the gentleman we were talking of came up to us; and, upon
the knight's asking him who preached to-morrow, for
it was Saturday night, told us the Bishop of St. Asaph
in the morning, and Dr. South in the afternoon. He
then showed us his list of preachers for the whole
year, where I saw with a great deal of pleasure Archbishop Tillotson, Bishop Saunderson, Dr. Barrow, Dr.
Calamy, with several living authors who have published discourses of practical divinity. I no sooner
saw this venerable man in the pulpit, but I very much
approved of my friend's insisting upon the qualifica-

tions of a good aspect and a clear voice; for I was so charmed with the gracefulness of his figure and delivery, as well as the discourses he pronounced, that I think I never passed any time more to my satisfaction. A sermon repeated after this manner is like the composition of a poet in the mouth of a graceful actor.

I could heartily wish that more of our country clergy would follow this example; and, instead of wasting their spirits in laborious compositions of their own, would endeavour after a handsome elocution, and all those other talents that are proper to enforce what has been penned by greater masters. This would not only be more easy to themselves, but more edifying to the people.

SIR ROGER'S SERVANTS

Æsopo ingentem statuam posuére Attici,
Servumque collocârunt æternâ in basi,
Patere honoris scirent ut cunctis viam.

PHÆDR., *Epilog.* 1, 2.

The Athenians erected a large statue to Æsop, and placed him, though a slave, on a lasting pedestal, to show that the way to honour lies open indifferently to all.

THE reception, manner of attendance, undisturbed freedom, and quiet, which I meet with here in the country has confirmed me in the opinion I always had, that the general corruption of manners in servants is owing to the conduct of masters. The aspect of every one in the family carries so much satisfaction that it appears he knows the happy lot which has befallen him in being a member of it. There is one particular which I have seldom seen but at Sir Roger's: It is usual in all other places that servants fly from the parts of the house through which their master is passing; on the contrary, here they industriously place themselves in his way; and it is on both sides, as it were, understood as a visit when the servants appear without calling. This proceeds from the humane and equal temper of the man of the house, who also perfectly well knows how to enjoy a great estate with such economy as ever to be much beforehand. This makes his own mind untroubled, and consequently unapt to vent peevish expressions, or give passionate or inconsistent orders, to those about him. Thus respect and love go together; and a certain cheerfulness in performance of their duty is the particular distinction of the lower part of this family. When a servant is called before his master, he does not come with an expectation to hear himself rated for some trivial fault, threatened to be stripped, or used with any other unbecoming language, which mean masters often give to worthy servants; but it is often to know what road he took that he came so readily back according to order; whether he passed by such a ground; if the old man who rents it is in good health; or whether he gave Sir Roger's love to him; or the like.

A man who preserves a respect founded on his benevolence to his dependents lives rather like a prince than a master in his family; his orders are received as favours rather than duties; and the distinction of approaching him is part of the reward for executing what is commanded by him.

There is another circumstance in which my friend excels in his management, which is the manner of rewarding his servants. He has ever been of opinion that giving his cast clothes to be worn by valets has a

very ill effect upon little minds, and creates a silly sense
of equality between the parties, in persons affected
only with outward things. I have heard him often
pleasant on this occasion, and describe a young gentleman abusing his man in that coat which a month or
two before was the most pleasing distinction he was
conscious of in himself. He would turn his discourse
still more pleasantly upon the ladies' bounties in this
kind; and I have heard him say he knew a fine woman
who distributed rewards and punishments in giving
becoming or unbecoming dresses to her maids.

But my good friend is above these little instances of
good-will in bestowing only trifles on his servants; a
good servant to him is sure of having it in his choice
very soon of being no servant at all. As I before
observed, he is so good a husband, and knows so
thoroughly that the skill of the purse is the cardinal
virtue of this life; I say he knows so well that frugality is the support of generosity that he can often
spare a large fine when a tenement falls, and give that
settlement to a good servant who has a mind to go into
the world, or make a stranger pay the fine to that servant, for his more comfortable maintenance, if he stays
in his service.

A man of honour and generosity considers it would
be miserable to himself to have no will but that of
another, though it were of the best person breathing,

and for that reason goes on as fast as he is able to put his servants into independent livelihoods. The greatest part of Sir Roger's estate is tenanted by persons who have served himself or his ancestors. It was to me extremely pleasant to observe the visitants from several parts to welcome his arrival into the country; and all the difference that I could take notice of between the late servants who came to see him, and those who stayed in the family, was, that these latter were looked upon as finer gentlemen and better courtiers.

This manumission and placing them in a way of livelihood, I look upon as only what is due to a good servant; which encouragement will make his successor be as diligent, as humble, and as ready, as he was. There is something wonderful in the narrowness of those minds which can be pleased and be barren of bounty to those who please them.

One might, on this occasion, recount the sense that great persons in all ages have had of the merit of their dependents, and the heroic services which men have done their masters in the extremity of their fortunes, and shown to their undone patrons that fortune was all the difference between them; but as I design this my speculation only as a gentle admonition to thankless masters, I shall not go out of the occurrences of common life, but assert it as a general observation, that I never saw, but in Sir Roger's family and one or two

more, good servants treated as they ought to be.   Sir
Roger's kindness extends to their children's children,
and this very morning he sent his coachman's grand-
son to prentice.   I shall conclude this paper with an
account of a picture in his gallery, where there are
many which will deserve my future observation.

At the very upper end of this handsome structure I
saw the portraiture of two young men standing in a
river: the one naked, the other in a livery.   The person
supported seemed half dead, but still so much alive as
to show in his face exquisite joy and love towards the
other.   I thought the fainting figure resembled my
friend Sir Roger; and looking at the butler who
stood by me for an account of it, he informed
me that the person in the livery was a servant
of Sir Roger's, who stood on the shore while his
master was swimming, and observing him taken with
some sudden illness, and sink under water, jumped in
and saved him.   He told me Sir Roger took off the
dress he was in as soon as he came home, and by a
great bounty at that time, followed by his favour ever
since, had made him master of that pretty seat which
we saw at a distance as we came to this house.   I remembered indeed Sir Roger said there lived a very
worthy gentleman, to whom he was highly obliged,
without mentioning anything further.   Upon my looking a little dissatisfied at some part of the picture, my

attendant informed me that it was against Sir Roger s will, and at the earnest request of the gentleman himself, that he was drawn in the habit in which he had saved his master.

WILL WIMBLE

Gratis anhelans, multa agendo nihil agens.
PHÆDR., *Fab.* v. 2.

Out of breath to no purpose, and very busy about nothing.

As I was yesterday morning walking with Sir Roger before his house, a country fellow brought him a huge fish, which, he told him, Mr. William Wimble had caught that very morning; and that he presented it with his service to him, and intended to come and dine with him. At the same time he delivered a letter, which my friend read to me as soon as the messenger left him.

"SIR ROGER,

"I desire you to accept of a jack, which is the best I have caught this season. I intend to come and stay with you a week, and see how the perch bite in the Black River. I observe with some concern the last time I saw you upon the bowling-green that your whip wanted a lash to it; I will bring half a dozen with me that I twisted last week, which I hope will serve you all the time you are in the country. I have not been out of the saddle for six days last past, having been at Eton with Sir John's eldest son. He takes to his learning hugely.

> "I am, Sir,
>> "Your humble servant.
>>> "WILL WIMBLE."

This extraordinary letter and message that accompanied it made me very curious to know the character and quality of the gentleman who sent them, which I found to be as follows :—Will Wimble is younger brother to a baronet, and descended of the ancient family of the Wimbles. He is now between forty and fifty; but being bred to no business and born to no estate, he generally lives with his elder brother as superintendent of his game. He hunts a pack of dogs better than any man in the country, and is very famous for finding out a hare. He is extremely well versed in all the little handicrafts of an idle man. He makes a May-fly to a miracle, and furnishes the whole country with angle-rods. As he is a good-natured, officious fellow, and very much esteemed upon account of his family, he is a welcome guest at every house, and keeps up a good correspondence among all the gentlemen about him. He carries a tulip root in his pocket from one to another, or exchanges a puppy between a couple of friends that live perhaps in the opposite sides of the county. Will is a particular favourite of all the young heirs, whom he frequently obliges with a net that he has weaved, or a setting-dog that he has made himself. He now and then presents a pair of garters of his own knitting to their mothers or sisters, and raises a great deal of mirth among them by inquiring as often as he meets them "how they wear!" These gentleman-like manufactures and obliging little humours make Will the darling of the country.

Sir Roger was proceeding in the character of him, when he saw him make up to us with two or three hazel twigs in his hand that he had cut in Sir Roger's woods, as he came through them, on his way to the house. I was very much pleased to observe on one side the hearty and sincere welcome with which Sir Roger received him, and on the other the secret joy which his guest discovered at sight of the good old knight. After the first salutes were over, Will desired Sir Roger to lend him one of his servants to carry a set of shuttlecocks he had with him in a little box to a lady that lived about a mile off, to whom it seems he had promised such a present for above this half year. Sir Roger's back was no sooner turned but honest Will began to tell me of a large cock pheasant that he had sprung in one of the neighbouring woods, with two or

three other adventures of the same nature. Odd and
uncommon characters are the game that I look for, and
most delight in; for which reason I was as much
pleased with the novelty of the person that talked to
me as he could be for his life with the springing of a
pheasant, and therefore listened to him with more than
ordinary attention.

In the midst of his discourse the bell rung to dinner,
where the gentleman I have been speaking of had the
pleasure of seeing the huge jack he had caught served
up for the first dish in a most sumptuous manner.
Upon our sitting down to it, he gave us a long account
how he had hooked it, played with it, foiled it, and at
length drew it out upon the bank, with several other
particulars that lasted all the first course. A dish of
wildfowl that came afterwards furnished conversation
for the rest of the dinner, which concluded with a late
invention of Will's for improving the quail-pipe.

Upon withdrawing into my room after dinner, I was
secretly touched with compassion towards the honest
gentleman that had dined with us; and could not but
consider, with a great deal of concern, how so good a
heart and such busy hands were wholly employed in
trifles; that so much humanity should be so little
beneficial to others, and so much industry so little ad-
vantageous to himself. The same temper of mind and
application to affairs might have recommended him to

the public esteem, and have raised his fortune in another station of life. What good to his country or himself might not a trader or a merchant have done with such useful though ordinary qualifications?

Will Wimble's is the case of many a younger brother of a great family, who had rather see their children starve like gentlemen than thrive in a trade or profession that is beneath their quality. This humour fills several parts of Europe with pride and beggary. It is the happiness of a trading nation like ours that the younger sons, though incapable of any liberal art or profession, may be placed in such a way of life as may perhaps enable them to vie with the best of their family. Accordingly we find several citizens that were launched into the world with narrow fortunes rising by an honest industry to greater estates than those of their elder brothers. It is not improbable but Will was formerly tried at divinity, law, or physic; and that, finding his genius did not lie that way, his parents gave him up at length to his own inventions.

But certainly, however improper he might have been for studies of a higher nature, he was perfectly well turned for the occupations of trade and commerce. As I think this is a point which cannot be too much inculcated, I shall desire my reader to compare what I have here written with what I have said in another speculation.

SIR ROGER'S ANCESTORS

—*Abnormis sapiens.*

HOR., *Sat.* ii. 2, 3.

Of plain good sense, untutored in the schools.

I WAS this morning walking in the gallery, when Sir
Roger entered at the end opposite to me, and, advancing
towards me, said he was glad to meet me among his
relations the De Coverleys, and hoped I liked the conversation of so much good company, who were as
silent as myself. I knew he alluded to the pictures,
and, as he is a gentleman who does not a little value
himself upon his ancient descent, I expected he would
give me some account of them. We were now arrived
at the upper end of the gallery, when the knight faced
towards one of the pictures, and as we stood before it,
he entered into the matter after his blunt way of saying things as they occur to his imagination, without
regular introduction, or care to preserve the appearance
of chain of thought.

" It is," said he, " worth while to consider the force of
dress, and how the persons of one age differ from those
of another, merely by that only. One may observe also
that the general fashion of one age has been followed

by one particular set of people in another, and by them preserved from one generation to another. Thus the vast jetting coat and small bonnet, which was the habit in Henry the Seventh's time, is kept on in the yeomen of the guard; not without a good and politic view, because they look a foot taller, and a foot and a half broader; besides that the cap leaves the face expanded, and consequently more terrible, and fitter to stand at the entrance of palaces.

" This predecessor of ours you see is dressed after this manner, and his cheeks would be no larger than mine were he in a hat as I am. He was the last man that won a prize in the tilt-yard, which is now a common street before Whitehall. You see the broken lance that lies there by his right foot. He shivered that lance of his adversary all to pieces; and bearing himself, look you, sir, in this manner, at the same time he came within the target of the gentleman who rode against him, and taking him with incredible force before him on the pommel of his saddle, he in that manner rid the tournament over with an air that showed he did it rather to perform the rule of the lists than expose his enemy; however it appeared he knew how to make use of a victory, and with a gentle trot he marched up to a gallery where their mistress sat, for they were rivals, and let him down with laudable courtesy and pardonable insolence. I don't know,

D—33

but it might be exactly where the coffee-house is
now.

"You are to know this my ancestor was not only of
a military genius, but fit also for the arts of peace, for
he played on the bass-viol as well as any gentleman at
court; you see where his viol hangs by his basket-hilt
sword. The action at the tilt-yard you may be sure
won the fair lady, who was a maid of honour, and the
greatest beauty of her time; here she stands the next
picture. You see, sir, my great-great-great-grand-
mother has on the new-fashioned petticoat, except that
the modern is gathered at the waist; my grandmother
appears as if she stood in a large drum, whereas the
ladies now walk as if they were in a go-cart. For all
this lady was bred at court, she became an excellent
country wife; she brought ten children; and when I
show you the library, you shall see in her own hand,
allowing for the difference of the language, the best
receipt now in England both for a hasty-pudding and
a white-pot.

"If you please to fall back a little, because it is
necessary to look at the three next pictures at one
view; these are three sisters. She on the right hand,
who is so very beautiful, died a maid; the next to her,
still handsomer, had the same fate, against her will;
this homely thing, in the middle, had both their portions added to her own, and was stolen by a neigh-

bouring gentleman, a man of stratagem and resolution, for he poisoned three mastiffs to come at her, and knocked down two deer-stealers in carrying her off. Misfortunes happen in all families. The theft of this romp, and so much money, was no great matter to our estate. But the next heir that possessed it was this soft gentleman, whom you see there. Observe the small buttons, the little boots, the laces, the slashes about his clothes, and above all the posture he is drawn in, which to be sure was his own choosing; you see he sits with one hand on a desk writing and looking as it were another way, like an easy writer or a sonnetteer. He was one of those that had too much wit to know how to live in the world; he was a man of no justice, but great good manners. He ruined everybody that had anything to do with him, but never said a rude thing in his life; the most indolent person in the world, he would sign a deed that passed away half his estate with his gloves on, but would not put on his hat before a lady if it were to save his country. He is said to be the first that made love by squeezing the hand. He left the estate with ten thousand pounds debt upon it; but, however, by all hands I have been informed that he was every way the finest gentleman in the world. That debt lay heavy on our house for one generation, but it was retrieved, by a gift from that honest man you see there. a citizen of our name, but nothing at all akin to us. I know Sir Andrew Freeport has said behind my back that this man was descended from one of the ten children of the maid of honour I showed you above; but it was never made out. We winked at the thing indeed, because money was wanting at that time."

Here I saw my friend a little embarrassed, and turned my face to the next portraiture.

Sir Roger went on with his account of the gallery in the following manner: "This man," pointing to him I looked at, "I take to be the honour of our house: Sir Humphry de Coverley. He was in his dealings as punctual as a tradesman, and as generous as a gentleman. He would have thought himself as much undone by breaking his word as if it were to be followed by bankruptcy. He served his country as knight of the shire to his dying day. He found it no easy matter to maintain an integrity in his words and actions, even in things that regarded the offices which were incumbent upon him, in the care of his own affairs and relations of life, and therefore dreaded, though he had great talents, to go into employments of state, where he must be exposed to the snares of ambition. Innocence of life and great ability were the distinguishing parts of his character; the latter, he had often observed, had led to the destruction of the 'former, and he used frequently to lament that great and good had not the same signification. He was an excellent husbandman, but had resolved not to exceed such a degree of wealth; all above it he bestowed in secret bounties many years after the sum he aimed at for his own use was attained. Yet he did not slacken his industry, but to a decent old age spent the life and fortune which was superfluous to himself in the service of his friends and neighbours."

Here we were called to dinner, and Sir Roger ended the discourse of this gentleman by telling me, as we followed the servant, that this his ancestor was a brave man, and narrowly escaped being killed in the civil wars; "for," said he, "he was sent out of the field upon a private message the day before the battle of Worcester." The whim of narrowly escaping by having been within a day of danger, with other matters above mentioned, mixed with good sense, left me at a loss whether I was more delighted with my friend's wisdom or simplicity.

NIGHT FEARS

Horror ubique animos, simul ipsa silentia terrent.
                    VIRG., *Æn.* ii. 755.

All things were full of horror and affright,
And dreadful even the silence of the night.
                              DRYDEN.

AT a little distance from Sir Roger's house, among
the ruins of an old abbey, there is a long walk of
aged elms, which are shot up so very high that when
one passes under them the rooks and crows that rest
upon the tops of them seem to be cawing in another
region.   I am very much delighted with this sort of
noise, which I consider as a kind of natural prayer to
that Being who supplies the wants of His whole creation, and who, in the beautiful language of the Psalms,
feedeth the young ravens that call upon Him.   I like
this retirement the better, because of an ill report it lies
under of being haunted; for which reason, as I have
been told in the family, no living creature ever walks
in it besides the chaplain.   My good friend the butler
desired me with a very grave face not to venture myself
in it after sunset, for that one of the footmen had been
almost frighted out of his wits by a spirit that appeared
to him in the shape of a black horse without a head;

to which he added that about a month ago one of the maids, coming home late that way with a pail of milk upon her head, heard such a rustling among the bushes that she let it fall.

I was taking a walk in this place last night between the hours of nine and ten, and could not but fancy it one of the most proper scenes in the world for a ghost to appear in. The ruins of the abbey are scattered up and down on every side, and half covered with ivy and elder bushes, the harbours of several solitary birds which seldom make their appearance till the dusk of the evening. The place was formerly a churchyard, and has still several marks in it of graves and burying places. There is such an echo among the old ruins and vaults that if you stamp but a little louder than ordinary you hear the sound repeated. At the same time, the walk of elms, with the croaking of the ravens which from time to time is heard from the tops of them, looks exceeding solemn and venerable. These objects naturally raise seriousness and attention ; and when night heightens the awfulness of the place, and pours out her supernumerary horrors upon everything in it I do not at all wonder that weak minds fill it with spectres and apparitions.

Mr. Locke, in his chapter of the Association of Ideas, has very curious remarks to show how, by the prejudice of education, one idea often introduces into

the mind a whole set that bear no resemblance to
one another in the nature of things. Among several
examples of this kind, he produces the following instance. " The ideas of goblins and sprites have really
no more to do with darkness than light ; yet let but a
foolish maid inculcate these often on the mind of a
child, and raise them there together, possibly he shall
never be able to separate them again so long as he
lives ; but darkness shall ever afterwards bring with it
those frightful ideas, and they shall be so joined that
he can no more bear the one than the other."

As I was walking in this solitude, where the dusk
of the evening conspired with so many other occasions
of terror, I observed a cow grazing not far from me,
which an imagination that was apt to startle might
easily have construed into a black horse without a
head ; and I daresay the poor footman lost his wits
upon some such trivial occasion.

My friend Sir Roger has often told me, with a great
deal of mirth, that at his first coming to his estate he
found three parts of his house altogether useless ; that
the best room in it had the reputation of being
haunted, and by that means was locked up ; that noises
had been heard in his long gallery, so that he could not
get a servant to enter it after eight o'clock at night ;
that the door of one of his chambers was nailed up,
because there went a story in the family that a butler

had formerly hanged himself in it; and that his mother, who lived to a great age, had shut up half the rooms in the house, in which either her husband, a son, or daughter, had died. The knight, seeing his habitation reduced to so small a compass, and himself in a manner shut out of his own house, upon the death of his mother ordered all the apartments to be flung open and exorcised by his chaplain, who lay in every room one after another, and by that means dissipated the fears which had so long reigned in the family.

I should not have been thus particular upon these ridiculous horrors did not I find them so very much prevail in all parts of the country. At the same time I think a person who is thus terrified with the imagination of ghosts and spectres much more reasonable than one who, contrary to the reports of all historians, sacred and profane, ancient and modern, and to the traditions of all nations, thinks the appearance of spirits fabulous and groundless. Could not I give myself up to this general testimony of mankind, I should to the relations of particular persons who are now living, and whom I cannot distrust in other matters of fact. I might here add that not only the historians, to whom we may join the poets, but likewise the philosophers of antiquity, have favoured this opinion. Lucretius himself, though by the course of his philosophy he was obliged to maintain that the soul did not exist

D*—33

separate from the body, makes no doubt of the reality
of apparitions, and that men have often appeared after
their death.   This I think very remarkable : he was
so pressed with the matter of fact, which he could not
have the confidence to deny, that he was forced to account for it by one of the most absurd unphilosophical
notions that was ever started.   He tells us that the
surfaces of all bodies are perpetually flying off from
their respective bodies, one after another; and that
these surfaces or thin cases that included each other
whilst they were joined in the body like the coats of
an onion are sometimes seen entire when they are
separated from it : by which means we often behold
the shapes and shadows of persons who are either dead
or absent.

I shall dismiss this paper with a story out of Jose-
phus, not so much for the sake of the story itself as
for the moral reflections with which the author con-
cludes it, and which I shall here set down in his own
words.   "Glaphyra, the daughter of King Archelaus,
after the death of her two first husbands, being married
to a third, who was brother to her first husband, and
so passionately in love with her that he turned off his
former wife to make room for this marriage, had a very
odd kind of dream.   She fancied that she saw her first
husband coming towards her, and that she embraced
him with great tenderness ; when in the midst of the

pleasure which she expressed at the sight of him, he reproached her after the following manner: 'Glaphyra,' says he, 'thou hast made good the old saying, that women are not to be trusted. Was not I the husband of thy virginity? Have I not children by thee? How couldst thou forget our loves so far as to enter into a second marriage, and after that into a third, nay to take for thy husband a man who has so shamelessly crept into the bed of his brother? However, for the sake of our past loves, I shall free thee from thy present reproach, and make thee mine for ever.' Glaphyra told this dream to several women of her acquaintance, and died soon after." I thought this story might not be impertinent in this place, wherein I speak of those kings. Besides that the example deserves to be taken notice of, as it contains a most certain proof of the immortality of the soul, and of Divine Providence. If any man thinks these facts incredible, let him enjoy his opinion to himself, but let him not endeavour to disturb the belief of others, who by instances of this nature are excited to the study of virtue.

A COUNTRY SUNDAY WITH SIR ROGER DE COVERLEY

'Αθανάτους μὲν πρῶτα θεοὺς, νόμῳ ὡς διάκειται,
Τιμᾷ—   PYTHAG.

First, in obedience to thy country's rites,
Worship th' immortal gods.

I AM always very well pleased with a country Sunday,
and think, if keeping holy the seventh day were only
a human institution, it would be the best method that
could have been thought of for the polishing and
civilising of mankind. It is certain the country people
would soon degenerate into a kind of savages and
barbarians were there not such frequent returns of a
stated time, in which the whole village meet together
with their best faces, and in their cleanliest habits, to
converse with one another upon indifferent subjects,
hear their duties explained to them, and join together
in adoration of the Supreme Being. Sunday clears
away the rust of the whole week, not only as it re-
freshes in their minds the notions of religion, but as
it puts both the sexes upon appearing in their most
agreeable forms, and exerting all such qualities as are
apt to give them a figure in the eye of the village. A

country fellow distinguishes himself as much in the churchyard, as a citizen does upon the 'Change, the whole parish-politics being generally discussed in that place either after sermon or before the bell rings.

My friend Sir Roger, being a good churchman, has beautified the inside of his church with several texts of his own choosing. He has likewise given a handsome pulpit cloth, and railed in the communion-table at his own expense. He has often told me that at his coming to his estate he found his parishioners very irregular; and that, in order to make them kneel and join in the responses, he gave every one of them a hassock and a common Prayer-book; and at the same time employed an itinerant singing-master, who goes about the country for that purpose, to instruct them rightly in the tunes of the Psalms; upon which they now very much value themselves, and indeed outdo most of the country churches that I have ever heard.

As Sir Roger is landlord to the whole congregation, he keeps them in very good order, and will suffer nobody to sleep in it besides himself; for if by chance he has been surprised into a short nap at sermon, upon recovering out of it he stands up and looks about him, and if he sees anybody else nodding, either wakes them himself or sends his servant to them. Several other of the old knight's particularities break out upon these occasions. Sometimes he will be lengthening out a verse in the singing Psalms half a minute after the rest of the congregation have done with it ; sometimes when he is pleased with the matter of his devotion, he pronounces amen three or four times to the same prayer ; and sometimes stands up when everybody else is upon their knees, to count the congregation, or see if any of his tenants are missing.

I was yesterday very much surprised to hear my old friend in the midst of the service calling out to one John Matthews to mind what he was about, and not disturb the congregation. This John Matthews, it seems, is remarkable for being an idle fellow, and at that time was kicking his heels for his diversion. This authority of the knight, though exerted in that odd manner which accompanies him in all circumstances of life, has a very good effect upon the parish, who are not polite enough to see anything ridiculous in his behaviour ; besides that the general good sense and worthiness of his character make his friends observe these little singularities as foils that rather set off than blemish his good qualities.

As soon as the sermon is finished, nobody presumes to stir till Sir Roger is gone out of the church. The knight walks down from his seat in the chancel between a double row of his tenants that stand bowing to him on each side ; and every now and then inquires how such a one's wife, or mother, or son, or father, do, whom he does not see at church; which is understood as a secret reprimand to the person that is absent.

The chaplain has often told me that upon a catechising day, when Sir Roger has been pleased with a boy that answers well, he has ordered a Bible to be given him next day for his encouragement; and sometimes accompanies it with a flitch of bacon to his mother. Sir Roger has likewise added five pounds a year to the clerk's place; and, that he may encourage the young fellows to make themselves perfect in the Church service, has promised, upon the death of the present incumbent, who is very old, to bestow it according to merit.

The fair understanding between Sir Roger and his chaplain, and their mutual concurrence in doing good, is the more remarkable, because the very next village is famous for the differences and contentions that rise between the parson and the squire, who live in a perpetual state of war. The parson is always preaching at the squire; and the squire, to be revenged on the parson, never comes to church. The squire has made all his tenants atheists and tithe-stealers; while the parson instructs them every Sunday in the dignity of his order, and insinuates to them almost in every sermon that he is a better man than his patron. In short, matters are come to such an extremity that the squire has not said his prayers either in public or private this half year, and that the parson threatens him, if he does not mend his manners, to pray for him in the face of the whole congregation.

Feuds of this nature, though too frequent in the country, are very fatal to the ordinary people; who are so used to be dazzled with riches that they pay as much deference to the understanding of a man of an estate, as of a man of learning; and are very hardly brought to regard any truth, how important soever it may be, that is preached to them, when they know there are several men of five hundred a year who do not believe it.

SIR ROGER IN LOVE: THE PERVERSE WIDOW

—Hærent infixi pectore vultus.
                    VIRG., *Æn.* iv. 4.

Her looks were deep imprinted in his heart.

IN my first description of the company in which I pass most of my time, it may be remembered that I mentioned a great affliction which my friend Sir Roger had met with in his youth, which was no less than a disappointment in love. It happened this evening that we fell into a very pleasing walk at a distance from his house. As soon as we came into it, " It is," quoth the good old man, looking round him with a smile, " very hard that any part of my land should be settled upon one who has used me so ill as the perverse widow did; and yet I am sure I could not see a sprig of any bough of this whole walk of trees, but I should reflect upon her and her severity. She has certainly the finest hand of any woman in the world. You are to know this was the place wherein I used to muse upon her; and by that custom I can never come into it, but the same tender sentiments revive in my mind as if I had actually walked with that beautiful creature under these shades. I have been fool enough to carve her name on the bark of several of these trees ; so unhappy is the condition of men in love to attempt the removing of their passion by the methods which serve only to imprint it deeper. She has certainly the finest hand of any woman in the world."

Here followed a profound silence ; and I was not displeased to observe my friend falling so naturally into a discourse, which I had ever before taken notice he industriously avoided. After a very long pause, he entered upon an account of this great circumstance in his life with an air which I thought raised my idea of him above what I had ever had before ; and gave me the picture of that cheerful mind of his before it received that stroke which has ever since affected his words and actions.   But he went on as follows :

"I came to my estate in my twenty-second year, and resolved to follow the steps of the most worthy of my ancestors who have inhabited this spot of earth before me, in all the methods of hospitality and good neighbourhood, for the sake of my fame; and in country sports and recreations, for the sake of my health.   In my twenty-third year, I was obliged to serve as sheriff of the county; and in my servants, officers, and whole equipage, indulged the pleasure of a young man, who did not think ill of his own person, in taking that public occasion of showing my figure and behaviour to advantage.   You may easily imagine to yourself what appearance I made, who am pretty tall, rode well, and was very well dressed, at the head of a whole county, with music before me, a feather in my hat, and my horse well bitted.   I can assure you I was not a little pleased with the kind looks and glances I had from all the balconies and windows as I rode to the hall where the assizes were held.   But when I came there, a beautiful creature in a widow's habit sat in court to hear the event of a cause concerning her dower.   This commanding creature, who was born for the destruction of all who beheld her, put on such a resignation in her countenance, and bore the whispers of all around the court with such a pretty uneasiness, I warrant you,

and then recovered herself from one eye to another,
till she was perfectly confused by meeting something
so wistful in all she encountered, that at last, with
a murrain to her, she cast her bewitching eye upon
me. I no sooner met it but I bowed, like a great surprised booby; and, knowing her cause to be the first
which came on, I cried, like a captivated calf as I
was, ' Make way for the defendant's witnesses.' This
sudden partiality made all the county immediately see
the sheriff also was become a slave to the fine widow.
During the time her cause was upon trial, she behaved
herself, I warrant you, with such a deep attention to
her business, took opportunities to have little billets
handed to her counsel, then would be in such a pretty
confusion, occasioned, you must know, by acting
before so much company, that not only I, but the
whole court, was prejudiced in her favour; and all
that the next heir to her husband had to urge was
thought so groundless and frivolous that when it
came to her counsel to reply, there was not half so
much said as every one besides in the court thought
he could have urged to her advantage. You must
understand, sir, this perverse woman is one of those
unaccountable creatures that secretly rejoice in the
admiration of men, but indulge themselves in no
further consequences. Hence it is that she has ever
had a train of admirers, and she removes from her

slaves in town to those in the country according to the seasons of the year. She is a reading lady, and far gone in the pleasures of friendship. She is always accompanied by a confidant who is witness to her daily protestations against our sex, and consequently a bar to her first steps towards love, upon the strength of her own maxims and declarations.

"However, I must needs say, this accomplished mistress of mine has distinguished me above the rest, and has been known to declare Sir Roger de Coverley was the tamest and most human of all the brutes in the country. I was told she said so by one who thought he rallied me; but upon the strength of this slender encouragement of being thought least detestable, I made new liveries, new-paired my coach-horses, sent them all to town to be bitted, and taught to throw their legs well, and move all together, before I pretended to cross the country, and wait upon her. As soon as I thought my retinue suitable to the character of my fortune and youth, I set out from hence to make my addresses. The particular skill of this lady has ever been to inflame your wishes, and yet command respect. To make her mistress of this art, she has a greater share of knowledge, wit, and good sense than is usual even among men of merit. Then she is beautiful beyond the race of women. If you won't let her go on with a certain artifice with her eyes and the skill of beauty, she will arm herself with her real charms, and strike you with admiration instead of desire. It is certain that if you were to behold the whole woman, there is that dignity in her aspect, that composure in her motion, that complacency in her manner, that if her form makes you hope, her merit makes you fear. But then again she is such a desperate scholar that no country gentleman can approach her without being a jest. As I was going to tell you, when I came to her house, I was admitted to her presence with great civility ; at the same time she placed herself to be first seen by me in such an attitude as I think you call the posture of a picture, that she discovered new charms, and I at last came towards her with such an awe as made me speechless. This she no sooner observed but she made her advantage of it, and began a discourse to me concerning love and honour, as they both are followed by pretenders, and the real votaries to them. When she discussed these points in a discourse, which I verily believe was as learned as the best philosopher in Europe could possibly make, she asked me whether she was so happy as to fall in with my sentiments on these important particulars. Her confidant sat by her, and, upon my being in the last confusion and silence, this malicious aid of hers, turning to her, says, 'I am very glad to observe Sir Roger pauses upon

this subject, and seems resolved to deliver all his
sentiments upon the matter when he pleases to speak.'
They both kept their countenances, and after I had sat
half an hour meditating how to behave before such
profound casuists, I rose up and took my leave.
Chance has since that time thrown me very often in
her way, and she as often has directed a discourse to
me which I do not understand. This barbarity has
kept me ever at a distance from the most beautiful
object my eyes ever beheld. It is thus also she deals
with all mankind; and you must make love to her, as
you would conquer the Sphinx, by posing her. But
were she like other women, and that there were any
talking to her, how constant must the pleasure of that
man be who could converse with a creature.——But,
after all, you may be sure her heart is fixed on some
one or other; and yet I have been credibly informed—
but who can believe half that is said?—after she had
done speaking to me, she put her hand to her bosom,
and adjusted her tucker. Then she cast her eyes a
little down upon my beholding her too earnestly.
They say she sings excellently: her voice in her
ordinary speech has something in it inexpressibly
sweet. You must know I dined with her at a public
table the day after I first saw her, and she helped me
to some tansy in the eye of all the gentlemen in the
country. She has certainly the finest hand of any

woman in the world. I can assure you, sir, were you to behold her, you would be in the same condition; for as her speech is music, her form is angelic. But I find I grow irregular while I am talking of her; but indeed it would be stupidity to be unconcerned at such perfection. Oh, the excellent creature! she is as inimitable to all women as she is inaccessible to all men —— "

I found my friend begin to rave, and insensibly led him towards the house that we might be joined by some other company; and am convinced that the widow is the secret cause of all that inconsistency which appears in some parts of my friend's discourse; though he has so much command of himself as not directly to mention her, yet according to that of Martial, which one knows not how to render into English, *dum tacet, hanc loquitur*; I shall end this paper with that whole epigram, which represents with much humour my honest friend's condition:

> *Quidquid agit Rufus, nihil est nisi Nœvia Rufo,*
> *Si gaudet, si flet, si tacet, hanc loquitur :*
> *Cœnat, propinat, poscit, negat, innuit, una est*
> *Nœvia ; si non sit Nœvia, mutus erit.*
> *Scriberet hesternâ patri cùm luce salutem,*
> *Nœvia lux, inquit. Nœvia! lumen, ave.*
>
> *Epig.* i 69.

Let Rufus weep, rejoice, stand, sit, or walk,
Still he can nothing but of Nævia talk;

Let him eat, drink, ask questions or dispute,
Still he must speak of Nævia, or be mute.
He writ to his father, ending with this line
I am, my lovely Nævia, ever thine.

EXERCISE: SIR ROGER AS SPORTSMAN

—Ut sit mens sana in corpore sano,
Orandum est.   JUV., *Sat.* x. 356.

Pray for a sound mind in a sound body.

BODILY labour is of two kinds, either that which a
man submits to for his livelihood, or that which he
undergoes for his pleasure. The latter of them generally changes the name of labour for that of exercise,
but differs only from ordinary labour as it rises from
another motive.

A country life abounds in both these kinds of labour,
and for that reason gives a man a greater stock of
health, and consequently a more perfect enjoyment
of himself, than any other way of life. I consider
the body as a system of tubes and glands, or, to use
a more rustic phrase, a bundle of pipes and strainers,
fitted to one another after so wonderful a manner
as to make a proper engine for the soul to work with.
This description does not only comprehend the bowels,

bones, tendons, veins, nerves, and arteries, but every muscle and every ligature, which is a composition of fibres, that are so many imperceptible tubes or pipes, interwoven on all sides with invisible glands or strainers.

This general idea of a human body, without considering it in the niceties of anatomy, lets us see how absolutely necessary labour is for the right preservation of it. There must be frequent motions and agitations to mix, digest, and separate the juices contained in it, as well as to clear and cleanse that infinitude of pipes and strainers of which it is composed, and to give their solid parts a more firm and lasting tone. Labour or exercise ferments the humours, casts them into their proper channels, throws off redundancies, and helps nature in those secret distributions, without which the body cannot subsist in its vigour, nor the soul act with cheerfulness.

I might here mention the effects which this has upon all the faculties of the mind, by keeping the understanding clear, the imagination untroubled, and refining those spirits that are necessary for the proper exertion of our intellectual faculties, during the present laws of union between soul and body. It is to a neglect in this particular that we must ascribe the spleen, which is so frequent in men of studious and sedentary tempers, as well as the vapours to which those of the other sex are so often subject.

Had not exercise been absolutely necessary for our well-being, Nature would not have made the body so proper for it, by giving such an activity to the limbs, and such a pliancy to every part as necessarily produce those compressions, extensions, contortions, dilatations, and all other kinds of motions that are necessary for the preservation of such a system of tubes and glands as has been before mentioned. And, that we might not want inducements to engage us in such an exercise of the body as is proper for its welfare, it is so ordered that nothing valuable can be procured without it. Not to mention riches and honour, even food and raiment are not to be come at without the toil of the hands and sweat of the brows. Providence furnishes materials, but expects that we should work them up ourselves. The earth must be laboured before it gives its increase, and when it is forced into its several products, how many hands must they pass through before they are fit for use! Manufactures, trade, and agriculture, naturally employ more than nineteen parts of the species in twenty; and as for those who are not obliged to labour, by the condition in which they are born, they are more miserable than the rest of mankind, unless they indulge themselves in that voluntary labour which goes by the name of exercise.

My friend Sir Roger has been an indefatigable man

in business of this kind, and has hung several parts of his house with the trophies of his former labours. The walls of his great hall are covered with the horns of several kinds of deer that he has killed in the chase, which he thinks the most valuable furniture of his house, as they afford him frequent topics of discourse, and show that he has not been idle. At the lower end of the hall is a large otter's skin stuffed with hay, which his mother ordered to be hung up in that manner, and the knight looks upon with great satisfaction, because it seems he was but nine years old when his dog killed him. A little room adjoining to the hall is a kind of arsenal filled with guns of several sizes and inventions, with which the knight has made great havoc in the woods, and destroyed many thousands of pheasants, partridges, and woodcocks. His stable-doors are patched with noses that belonged to foxes of the knight's own hunting down. Sir Roger showed me one of them that for distinction sake has a brass nail stuck through it, which cost him about fifteen hours' riding, carried him through half a dozen counties, killed him a brace of geldings, and lost above half his dogs. This the knight looks upon as one of the greatest exploits of his life. The perverse widow, whom I have given some account of, was the death of several foxes; for Sir Roger has told me that in the course of his amours he patched the western door of his stable. Whenever the widow was cruel, the foxes were sure to pay for it. In proportion as his passion for the widow abated, and old age came on, he left off fox-hunting; but a hare is not yet safe that sits within ten miles of his house.

There is no kind of exercise which I would so recommend to my readers of both sexes as this of riding, as there is none which so much conduces to health, and is every way accommodated to the body, according to the idea which I have given of it. Doctor Sydenham is very lavish in its praises; and if the English reader would see the mechanical effects of it described at length, he may find them in a book published not many years since under the title of the "Medicina Gymnastica." For my own part, when I am in town, for want of these opportunities, I exercise myself an hour every morning upon a dumb bell that is placed in a corner of my room, and it pleases me the more because it does everything I require of it in the most profound silence. My landlady and her daughters are so well acquainted with my hours of exercise that they never come into my room to disturb me whilst I am ringing.

When I was some years younger than I am at present, I used to employ myself in a more laborious diversion, which I learned from a Latin Treatise of Exercises that is written with great erudition. It is there called the σκιομαχία, or the fighting with a man's own shadow, and consists in the brandishing of two short sticks grasped in each hand, and loaded with plugs of lead at either end. This opens the chest, exercises the limbs, and gives a man all the pleasure of boxing without the blows. I could wish that several learned men would lay out that time which they employ in controversies and disputes about nothing in this method of fighting with their own shadows. It might conduce very much to evaporate the spleen, which makes them uneasy to the public as well as to themselves.

To conclude. As I am a compound of soul and body, I consider myself as obliged to a double scheme of duties; and I think I have not fulfilled the business of the day when I do not thus employ the one in labour and exercise as well as the other in study and contemplation.

- -

MOLL WHITE

.

—Ipsi sibi somnia finount.

VIRG., *Ecl.* viii. 108.

With voluntary dreams they cheat their minds.

THERE are some opinions in which a man should stand neuter, without engaging his assent to one side or the other. Such a hovering faith as this, which refuses to settle upon any determination, is absolutely necessary in a mind that is careful to avoid errors and pre-possessions. When the arguments press equally on both sides in matters that are indifferent to us, the safest method is to give up ourselves to neither.

It is with this temper of mind that I consider the subject of witchcraft. When I hear the relations that are made from all parts of the world, not only from Norway and Lapland, from the East and West Indies, but from every particular nation in Europe, I cannot forbear thinking that there is such an intercourse and commerce with evil spirits as that which we express by the name of witchcraft. But when I consider that the ignorant and credulous parts of the world abound most in these relations, and that the persons among us, who are supposed to engage in such an infernal com-merce, are people of a weak understanding and crazed imagination, and at the same time reflect upon the many impostures and delusions of this nature that have been detected in all ages, I endeavour to suspend my belief till I hear more certain accounts than any which have yet come to my knowledge. In short, when I consider the question, whether there are such persons in the world as those we call witches, my mind is divided between two opposite opinions, or rather, to speak my thoughts freely, I believe in general that there is, and has been, such a thing as witchcraft, but at the same time can give no credit to any particular instance of it.

I am engaged in this speculation by some occurrences that I met with yesterday, which I shall give my reader an account of at large. As I was walking with my friend Sir Roger, by the side of one of his woods, an old woman applied herself to me for my charity. Her dress and figure put me in mind of the following description in Otway :

> In a close lane, as I pursued my journey,
> I spied a wrinkled hag, with age grown double,
> Picking dry sticks, and mumbling to herself.
> Her eyes with scalding rheum were galled and red ;
> Cold palsy shook her head ; her hands seemed withered ;
> And on her crooked shoulders had she wrapt
> The tattered remnant of an old striped hanging,
> Which served to keep her carcase from the cold :
> So there was nothing of a piece about her.
> Her lower weeds were all o'er coarsely patched
> With different coloured rags, black, red, white, yellow,
> And seemed to speak variety of wretchedness.

As I was musing on this description, and comparing it with the object before me, the knight told me that this very old woman had the reputation of a witch all over the country, that her lips were observed to be always in motion, and that there was not a switch about her house which her neighbours did not believe had carried her several hundreds of miles. If she chanced to stumble, they always found sticks or straws that lay in the figure of a cross before her. If she made any mistake at church, and cried "Amen" in a wrong place, they never failed to conclude that she was saying her prayers backwards. There was not a maid in the parish that would take a pin of her, though she should offer a bag of money with it. She goes by the name of Moll White, and has made the country ring with several imaginary exploits which are palmed upon her. If the dairymaid does not make her butter to come so soon as she would have it, Moll White is at the bottom of the churn. If a horse sweats in the stable, Moll White has been upon his back. If a hare makes an unexpected escape from the hounds, the huntsman curses Moll White. "Nay," says Sir Roger, "I have known the master of the pack, upon such an occasion, send one of his servants to see if Moll White had been out that morning."

This account raised my curiosity so far that I begged my friend Sir Roger to go with me into her hovel, which stood in a solitary corner under the side of the wood. Upon our first entering, Sir Roger winked to me, and pointed at something that stood behind the door, which, upon looking that way, I found to be an old broom-staff. At the same time, he whispered me in the ear to take notice of a tabby cat that sat in the chimney corner, which, as the knight told me, lay under as bad a report as Moll White herself; for besides that Moll is said often to accompany her in the same shape, the cat is reported to have spoken twice or thrice in her life, and to have played several pranks above the capacity of an ordinary cat.

I was secretly concerned to see human nature in so much wretchedness and disgrace, but at the same time could not forbear smiling to hear Sir Roger, who is a little puzzled about the old woman, advising her, as a justice of peace, to avoid all communication with the devil, and never to hurt any of her neighbours' cattle. We concluded our visit with a bounty which was very acceptable.

In our return home, Sir Roger told me that old Moll had been often brought before him for making children spit pins, and giving maids the nightmare; and that the country people would be tossing her into a pond and trying experiments with her every day if it was not for him and his chaplain.

I have since found upon inquiry that Sir Roger was several times staggered with the reports that had been brought him concerning this old woman, and would frequently have bound her over to the county sessions had not his chaplain, with much ado, persuaded him to the contrary.

E—33

I have been the more particular in this account because I hear there is scarce a village in England that has not a Moll White in it. When an old woman begins to dote, and grow chargeable to a parish, she is generally turned into a witch, and fills the whole country with extravagant fancies, imaginary distempers, and terrifying dreams. In the meantime, the poor wretch that is the innocent occasion of so many evils begins to be frightened at herself, and sometimes confesses secret commerces and familiarities that her imagination forms in a delirious old age. This frequently cuts off charity from the greatest objects of compassion, and inspires people with a malevolence towards those poor decrepit parts of our species, in whom human nature is defaced by infirmity and dotage.

THE WORLD'S OPINION : SIR ROGER AMONG HIS NEIGHBOURS

Comes jucundus in via pro vehiculo est.

PUBL., *Syr. Frag.*

An agreeable companion upon the road is as good as a coach.

A MAN'S first care should be to avoid the reproaches of his own heart; his next, to escape the censures of the world. If the last interferes with the former, it ought to be entirely neglected; but otherwise there cannot be a greater satisfaction to an honest mind than to see those approbations which it gives itself seconded by the applauses of the public. A man is more sure of his conduct when the verdict which he passes upon his own behaviour is thus warranted and confirmed by the opinion of all that know him.

My worthy friend Sir Roger is one of those who is not only at peace within himself, but beloved and esteemed by all about him. He receives a suitable tribute for his universal benevolence to mankind in the returns of affection and good-will which are paid him by every one that lives within his neighbourhood. I lately met with two or three odd instances of that general respect which is shown to the good old knight. He would needs carry Will Wimble and myself with him to the country assizes. As we were upon the road, Will Wimble joined a couple of plain men who rode before us, and conversed with them for some time, during which my friend Sir Roger acquainted me with their characters.

" The first of them," says he, " that has a spaniel by his side, is a yeoman of about a hundred pounds a year, an honest man. He is just within the Game Act, and qualified to kill a hare or a pheasant. He knocks down a dinner with his gun twice or thrice a week ; and by that means lives much cheaper than those who have not so good an estate as himself.   He would be a good neighbour if he did not destroy so many partridges. In short, he is a very sensible man; shoots flying; and has been several times foreman of the petty jury.

" The other that rides along with him is Tom Touchy, a fellow famous for ' taking the law ' of everybody. There is not one in the town where he lives that he has not sued at a quarter sessions.   The rogue had once the impudence to go to law with the widow.   His head is full of costs, damages, and ejectments.   He plagued a couple of honest gentlemen so long for a trespass in breaking one of his hedges, till he was forced to sell the ground it inclosed to defray the charges of the prosecution; his father left him fourscore pounds a year; but he has cast and been cast so often that he is not now worth thirty.   I suppose he is going upon the old business of the willow-tree."

As Sir Roger was giving me this account of Tom Touchy, Will Wimble and his two companions stopped short till we came up to them.   After having paid their respects to Sir Roger, Will told him that Mr. Touchy and he must appeal to him upon a dispute that arose between them.   Will it seems had been giving his fellow-travellers an account of his angling one day in such a hole, when Tom Touchy, instead of hearing out his story, told him that Mr. Such a One, if he pleased, might "take the law of him" for fishing in that part of the river. My friend Sir Roger heard them both upon a round trot; and after having paused some time told them, with the air of a man who would not give his judgment rashly, that "much might be' said on both sides." They were neither of them dissatisfied with the knight's determination, because neither of them found himself in the wrong by it. Upon which we made the best of our way to the assizes.

The court was sat before Sir Roger came; but notwithstanding all the justices had taken their places upon the bench, they made room for the old knight at the head of them; who for his reputation in the country took occasion to whisper in the judge's ear that he was glad his lordship had met with so much good weather in his circuit. I was listening to the proceedings of the court with much attention, and infinitely pleased with that great appearance and solemnity which so properly accompanies such a public administration of our laws, when, after about an hour's sitting, I observed to my great surprise, in the midst of a trial, that my friend Sir Roger was getting up to speak. I was in some pain for him, till I found he had acquitted himself of two or three sentences, with a look of much business and great intrepidity.

Upon his first rising, the court was hushed. and a

general whisper ran among the country people, that
Sir Roger "was up." The speech he made was so
little to the purpose that I shall not trouble my readers
with an account of it; and I believe was not so much
designed by the knight himself to inform the court as
to give him a figure in my eye, and keep up his credit
in the country.

I was highly delighted, when the court rose, to see
the gentlemen of the country gathering about my old
friend, and striving who should compliment him most;
at the same time that the ordinary people gazed upon
him at a distance, not a little admiring his courage
that was not afraid to speak to the judge.

In our return home we met with a very odd accident, which I cannot forbear relating, because it shows
how desirous all who know Sir Roger are of giving
him marks of their esteem. When we were arrived
upon the verge of his estate, we stopped at a little inn
to rest ourselves and our horses. The man of the house
had it seems been formerly a servant in the knight's
family; and, to do honour to his old master, had some
time since, unknown to Sir Roger, put him up in a
sign-post before the door; so that the knight's head
had hung out upon the road about a week before he
himself knew anything of the matter. As soon as Sir
Roger was acquainted with it, finding that his servant's
indiscretion proceeded wholly from affection and good-

will, he only told him that he had made him too high
a compliment; and, when the fellow seemed to think
that could hardly be, added, with a more decisive look,
that it was too great an honour for any man under a
duke; but told him at the same time that it might be
altered with a very few touches, and that he himself
would be at the charge of it. Accordingly they got a
painter by the knight's directions to add a pair of
whiskers to the face, and by a little aggravation of the
features to change it into the Saracen's Head. I should
not have known this story had not the innkeeper, upon
Sir Roger's alighting, told him in my hearing that his
honour's head was brought back last night with the
alterations that he had ordered to be made in it. Upon
this my friend, with his usual cheerfulness, related the
particulars above mentioned, and ordered the head to
be brought into the room. I could not forbear dis-
covering greater expressions of mirth than ordinary
upon the appearance of this monstrous face, under
which, notwithstanding it was made to frown and stare
in a most extraordinary manner, I could still discover
a distant resemblance of my old friend. Sir Roger,
upon seeing me laugh, desired me to tell him truly if I
thought it possible for people to know him in that
disguise. I at first kept my usual silence; but, upon
the knight's conjuring me to tell him whether it was not
still more like himself than a Saracen, I composed my

countenance in the best manner I could, and replied, "that much might be said on both sides."

These several adventures, with the knight's behaviour in them, gave me as pleasant a day as ever I met with in any of my travels.

PARTY SPIRIT

Ne, pueri, ne tanta animis assuescite bella ;
Neu patria validas in viscera vertite vires.

VIRG., *Æn.* vi. 832.

This thirst of kindred blood, my sons, detest,
Nor turn your force against your country's breast.

MY worthy friend Sir Roger, when we are talking of the malice of parties, very frequently tells us an accident that happened to him when he was a schoolboy, which was at a time when the feuds ran high between the Roundheads and Cavaliers. This worthy knight, being then but a stripling, had occasion to inquire which was the way to St. Anne's Lane, upon which the person whom he spoke to, instead of answering his question, called him a young Popish cur, and asked him who had made Anne a saint. The boy being in some confusion inquired of the next he met which was the way to Anne's Lane; but was called a prick-eared cur for his pains, and, instead of being shown the way, was told that she had been a saint before he was born, and would be one after he was hanged. "Upon this," says Sir Roger, "I did not think fit to repeat the former question, but, going into every lane of the neighbourhood, asked what they called the name of that lane." By which ingenious artifice he found out the place he inquired after without giving offence to any party. Sir Roger generally closes this narrative with reflections on the mischief that parties do in the country; how they spoil good neighbourhood, and make honest gentlemen hate one another; besides that they manifestly tend to the prejudice of the land-tax and the destruction of the game.

There cannot a greater judgment befall a country than such a dreadful spirit of division as rends a government into two distinct people, and makes them greater strangers and more averse to one another than if they were actually two different nations. The effects of such a division are pernicious to the last degree, not only with regard to those advantages which they give the common enemy, but to those private evils which they produce in the heart of almost every particular person. This influence is very fatal both to men's morals and their understandings; it sinks the virtue of a nation, and not only so, but destroys even common sense.

E*—33

GIPSIES

—*Semperque recentes*
Convectare juvat prædas, et vivere rapto.
VIRG., *Æn*. vii. 748.

A plund'ring race, still eager to invade,
On spoil they live, and make of theft a trade.

As I was yesterday riding out in the fields with my
friend Sir Roger, we saw at a little distance from us
a troop of gipsies. Upon the first discovery of them,
my friend was in some doubt whether he should not
exert the justice of the peace upon such a band of
lawless vagrants; but not having his clerk with him,
who is a necessary counsellor on these occasions, and
fearing that his poultry might fare the worse for it, he
let the thought drop, but at the same time gave me a
particular account of the mischiefs they do in the
country in stealing people's goods and spoiling their
servants. "If a stray piece of linen hangs upon a
hedge," says Sir Roger, "they are sure to have it; if
a hog loses his way in the fields, it is ten to one but
he becomes their prey; our geese cannot live in peace
for them; if a man prosecutes them with severity,
his hen-roost is sure to pay for it. They generally
straggle into these parts about this time of the year,

and set the heads of our servant-maids so agog for husbands that we do not expect to have any business done as it should be whilst they are in the country. I have an honest dairymaid who crosses their hands with a piece of silver every summer, and never fails being promised the handsomest young fellow in the parish for her pains. Your friend the butler has been fool enough to be seduced by them, and though he is sure to lose a knife, a fork, or a spoon every time his fortune is told him, he generally shuts himself up in the pantry with an old gipsy for above half an hour once in a twelvemonth. Sweethearts are the things they live upon, which they bestow very plentifully upon all those that apply themselves to them. You see now and then some handsome young jades among them; the sluts have very often white teeth and black eyes."

Sir Roger, observing that I listened with great attention to his account of a people who were so entirely new to me, told me that, if I would, they should tell us our fortunes. As I was very well pleased with the knight's proposal, we rode up and communicated our hands to them. A Cassandra of the crew, after having examined my lines very diligently, told me that I loved a pretty maid in a corner, that I was a good woman's man, with some other particulars which I do not think proper to relate. My friend Sir Roger alighted from

his horse, and exposing his palm to two or three that
stood by him, they crumpled it into all shapes, and
diligently scanned every wrinkle that could be made
in it; when one of them, who was older and more sun-
burnt than the rest, told him that he had a widow in
his line of life. Upon which the knight cried, "Go,
go, you are an idle baggage," and at the same time
smiled upon me. The gipsy, finding he was not displeased in his heart, told him, after a further inquiry
into his hand that his true-love was constant, and that
she should dream of him to-night. My old friend
cried "Pish," and bade her go on. The gipsy told
him that he was a bachelor, but would not be so long;
and that he was dearer to somebody than he thought.
The knight still repeated, "She was an idle baggage,"
and bid her go on. "Ah, master," says the gipsy,
"that roguish leer of yours makes a pretty woman's
heart ache; you ha'n't that simper about the mouth for
nothing." The uncouth gibberish with which all this
was uttered, like the darkness of an oracle, made us
the more attentive to it. To be short, the knight left
the money with her that he had crossed her hand with.
and got up again on his horse.

As we were riding away, Sir Roger told me that he
knew several sensible people who believed these gipsies
now and then foretold very strange things; and for
half an hour together appeared more jocund than

ordinary. In the height of his good-humour, meeting a common beggar upon the road, who was no conjurer, as he went to relieve him he found his pocket was picked, that being a kind of palmistry at which this race of vermin are very dexterous.

THE SPECTATOR RETURNS TO TOWN

-Ipsæ rursum concedite sylvæ.

VIRG., *Ecl.* x. 63.

Once more ye woods, adieu.

IT is usual for a man who loves country sports to pre-serve the game in his own grounds, and divert himself upon those that belong to his neighbour. My friend Sir Roger generally goes two or three miles from his house, and gets into the frontiers of his estate, before he beats about in search of a hare or partridge, on purpose to spare his own fields, where he is always sure of finding diversion, when the worst comes to the worst. By this means the breed about his house has time to increase and multiply, besides that the sport is the more agreeable where the game is the harder to come at, and where it does not lie so thick as to produce any perplexity or confusion in the pursuit. For these reasons, the country gentleman, like the fox, seldom preys near his own home.

In the same manner, I have made a month's excursion out of the town, which is the great field of game for sportsmen of my species, to try my fortune in the country, where I have started several subjects, and hunted them down with some pleasure to myself, and I hope to others. I am here forced to use a great deal of diligence before I can spring any thing to my mind, whereas in town, whilst I am following one character, it is ten to one but I am crossed in my way by another, and put up such a variety of odd creatures in both sexes, that they foil the scent of one another, and puzzle the chase. My greatest difficulty in the country is to find sport, and in town to choose it. In the mean time, as I have given a whole month's rest to the cities of London and Westminster, I promise myself abundance of new game upon my return thither.

It is indeed high time for me to leave the country, since I find the whole neighbourhood begin to grow very inquisitive after my name and character; my love of solitude, taciturnity, and particular way of life, having raised a great curiosity in all these parts.

The notions which have been framed of me are various; some look upon me as very proud, some as very modest, and some as very melancholy. Will

Wimble, as my friend the butler tells me, observing me very much alone, and extremely silent when I am in company, is afraid I have killed a man. The country people seem to suspect me for a conjurer; and some of them, hearing of the visit which I made to Moll White, will needs have it that Sir Roger has brought down a cunning man with him, to cure the old woman, and free the country from her charms. So that the character which I go under in part of the neighbourhood, is what they here call a White Witch.

A justice of peace, who lives about five miles off, and is not of Sir Roger's party, has, it seems, said twice or thrice at his table, that he wishes Sir Roger does not harbour a Jesuit in his house, and that he thinks the gentlemen of the country would do very well to make me give some account of myself.

On the other side, some of Sir Roger's friends are afraid the old knight is imposed upon by a designing fellow; and, as they have heard he converses very promiscuously when he is in town, do not know but he has brought down with him some discarded Whig, that is sullen, and says nothing, because he is out of place.

Such is the variety of opinions which are here entertained of me, so that I pass among some for a disaffected person, and among others for a popish priest; among some for a wizard, and among others for a murderer; and all this for no other reason that I can imagine, but because I do not hoot, and hollow, and make a noise. It is true, my friend Sir Roger tells them—" That it is my way," and that I am only a philosopher; but this will not satisfy them. They think there is more in me than he discovers, and that I do not hold my tongue for nothing.

For these and other reasons I shall set out for London to-morrow, having found by experience that the country is not a place for a person of my temper, who does not love ' jollity and what they call good neighbourhood. A man that is out of humour when an unexpected guests breaks in upon him, and does not care for sacrificing an afternoon to every chance-comer, that will be the master of his own time, and the pursuer of his own inclinations, makes but a very unsociable figure in this kind of life. I shall therefore retire into the town, if I may make use of that phrase, and get into the crowd again as fast as I can, in order to be alone. I can there raise what speculations I please upon others without being observed myself, and at the same time enjoy all the advantages of company with all the privileges of solitude. In the meanwhile, to finish the month, and conclude these my rural speculations, I shall here insert a letter from my friend Will Honeycomb, who has not lived a month for these forty years out of the smoke of London, and rallies me after his way upon my country life.

" DEAR SPEC,

"I suppose this letter will find thee picking of daisies, or smelling to a lock of hay, or passing away thy time in some innocent country diversion of the like nature. I have, however, orders from the club to summon thee up to town, being all of us cursedly afraid thou wilt not be able to relish our company after thy conversations with Moll White and Will Wimble. Pr'ythee don't send us up any more stories of a cock and a bull, nor frighten the town with spirits and witches. Thy speculations begin to smell confoundedly of woods and meadows. If thou dost not come up quickly, we shall conclude thou art in love with one of Sir Roger's dairy-maids. Service to knight. Sir Andrew is grown the cock of the club since he left us, and if he does not return quickly, will make every mother's son of us commonwealth's men.

" Dear Spec,

"Thine eternally,

" WILL HONEYCOMB."

Qui, aut tempus quid postulet non videt, aut plura loquitur, aut se ostentat, aut eorum quibuscum est rationem non habet, is ineptus esse dicitur.

TULL.

That man may be called impertinent who considers not the

circumstances of time, or engrosses the conversation, or makes himself the subject of his discourse, or pays no regard to the company he is in.

HAVING notified to my good friend Sir Roger that I should set out for London the next day, his horses were ready at the appointed hour in the evening; and, attended by one of his grooms, I arrived at the county town at twilight, in order to be ready for the stage-coach the day following. As soon as we arrived at the inn, the servant who waited upon me inquired of the chamberlain in my hearing what company he had for the coach? The fellow answered, "Mrs. Betty Arable, the great fortune, and the widow her mother; a re-cruiting officer, who took a place because they were to go, young Squire Quickset, her cousin, that her mother wished her to be married to; Ephraim the quaker, her guardian; and a gentleman that had studied himself dumb from Sir Roger de Coverley's." I observed, by what he said of myself, that according to his office he dealt much in intelligence; and doubted not but there was some foundation for his reports of the rest of the company, as well as for the whimsical account he gave of me. The next morning at day-break we were all called; and I, who know my own natural shyness, and endeavour to be as little liable to be disputed with as possible, dressed immediately, that I might make no one wait. The first preparation for our setting out was, that the captain's half pike was placed near the coachman, and a drum behind the coach. In the mean time, the drummer, the captain's equipage, was very loud, " that none of the captain's things should be placed so as to be spoiled;" upon which his cloak-bag was fixed in the seat of the coach; and the captain himself, according to a frequent, though invidious, behaviour of military men, ordered his man to look sharp, that none but one of the ladies should have the place he had taken fronting the coach-box.

We were in some little time fixed in our seats, and sat with that dislike which people not too good-natured usually conceive of each other at first sight. The coach jumbled us insensibly into some sort of familiarity: and we had not moved about two miles, when the widow asked the captain what success he had in his recruiting? The officer, with a frankness he believed very graceful, told her that indeed he had but very little luck, and had suffered much by desertion, therefore should be glad to end his warfare in the service of her or her fair daughter. "In a word," continued he, "I am a soldier, and to be plain is my character: you see me, madam, young, sound and impudent; take me yourself, widow, or give me to her, I will be wholly at your disposal. I am a soldier of fortune, ha!" This was followed by a vain laugh of his own, and a deep silence of all the rest of the company.

I had nothing left for it but to fall fast asleep, which I
did with all speed. " Come," said he, " resolve upon it,
we will make a wedding at the next town : we will wake
this pleasant companion, who is fallen asleep, to be the
brideman ; and," giving the quaker a clap on the knee,
he concluded, " this sly saint, who I'll warrant under-
stands what's what as well as you or I, widow, shall give
the bride as father." The quaker, who happened to be a
man of smartness, answered, " Friend, I take it in good
part that thou hast given me the authority of a father
over this comely and virtuous child; and I must assure
thee, that if I have the giving her, I shall not bestow
her on thee. Thy mirth, friend, savoureth of folly :
thou art a person of a light mind; thy drum is a type
of thee, it soundeth because it is empty. Verily, it
is not from thy fulness, but thy emptiness, that thou
hast spoken this day. Friend, friend, we have hired
this coach in partnership with thee, to carry us to the
great city ; we cannot go any other way. This worthy
mother must hear thee if thou wilt needs utter thy
follies ; we cannot help it, friend, I say ; if thou wilt,
we must hear thee; but if thou wert a man of understanding thou wouldst not take advantage of thy
courageous countenance to abash us children of peace.
Thou art, thou sayest, a soldier ; give quarter to us,
who cannot resist thee. Why didst thou fleer at our
friend, who feigned himself asleep ? He said nothing ;

but how dost thou know what he containeth? If thou speakest improper things in the hearing of this virtuous young virgin, consider it as an outrage against a distressed person that cannot get from thee : to speak indiscreetly what we are obliged to hear, by being hasped up with thee in this public vehicle, is in some degree assaulting on the high round.''

Here Ephraim paused, and the captain with a happy and uncommon impudence, which can be convicted and support itself at the same time, cries, '' Faith, friend, I thank thee; I should have been a little impertinent if thou hadst not reprimanded me. Come, thou art, I see, a smoky old fellow, and I will be very orderly the ensuing part of the journey. I was going to give myself airs, but, ladies, I beg pardon.''

The captain was so little out of humour, and our company was so far from being soured by this little ruffle, that Ephraim and he took a particular delight in being agreeable to each other for the future; and assumed their different provinces in the conduct of the company. Our reckonings, apartments, and accommodation fell under Ephraim; and the captain looked to all disputes on the road, as the good behaviour of our coachman, and the right we had of taking place, as going to London, of all vehicles coming from thence. The occurrences we met with were ordinary, and very little happened which could enter-

tain by the relation of them : but when I considered
the company we were in, I took it for no small good-
fortune that the whole journey was not spent in
impertinences, which to one part of us might be an
entertainment, to the other a suffering.   What, therefore, Ephraim said when we were almost arrived at
London, had to me an air not only of good understanding,
but good breeding.   Upon the young lady's expressing
her satisfaction in the journey, and declaring how delightful it had been to her, Ephraim delivered himself
as follows : " There is no ordinary part of human life
which expresseth so much a good mind, and a right
inward man, as his behaviour upon meeting with
strangers, especially such as may seem the most un-
suitable companions to him : such a man, when he
falleth in the way with persons of simplicity and innocence, however knowing he may be in the ways of men,
will not vaunt himself thereof, but will the rather hide
his superiority to them, that he may not be painful
unto them.   My good friend," continued he, turning
to the officer, " thee and I are to part by and by, and
peradventure we may never meet again ; but be advised by a plain man ; modes and apparel are but trifles
to the real man, therefore do not think such a man as
thyself terrible for thy garb, nor such a one as me
contemptible for mine.   When two such as thee and I
meet, with affections as we ought to have towards each

other, thou shouldst rejoice to see my peaceable demeanour, and I should be glad to see thy strength and ability to protect me in it."

A DEBATE AT THE CLUB

Hæc memini, et victum frustrà contendere Thyrsin.
.VIRG., *Ecl.* vii. 69.

The whole debate in memory I retain,
When Thyrsis argued warmly, but in vain.   POPE.

THERE is scarce anything more common than animosities between parties that cannot subsist but by their agreement : this was well represented in the sedition of the members of the human body in the old Roman fable. It is often the case of lesser confederate states against a superior power, which are hardly held together, though their unanimity is necessary for their common safety; and this is always the case of the landed and trading interests of Great Britain : the trader is fed by the product of the land, and the landed man cannot be clothed but by the skill of the trader ; and yet those interests are ever jarring.

We had last winter an instance of this at our club, in Sir Roger de Coverley and Sir Andrew Freeport,

between whom there is generally a constant, though
friendly, opposition of opinions.   It happened that
one of the company, in an historical discourse, was
observing, that Carthaginian faith was a proverbial
phrase to intimate breach of leagues.   Sir Roger said
it could hardly be otherwise: that the Carthaginians
were the greatest traders in the world; and, as gain is
the chief end of such a people, they never pursue any
other: the means to it are never regarded: they will,
if it comes easily, get money honestly; but if not,
they will not scruple to attain it by fraud or cozenage:
and indeed, what is the whole business of the trader's
account, but to over-reach him who trusts to his
memory?   But were that not so, what can there great
and noble be expected from him whose attention is for
ever fixed upon balancing his books and watching over
his expenses?   And at best, let frugality and parsimony be the virtues of the merchant, how much is his
punctual dealing below a gentleman's charity to the
poor, or hospitality among his neighbours!

Captain Sentry observed Sir Andrew very diligent
in hearing Sir Roger, and had a mind to turn the discourse, by taking notice in general, from the highest
to the lowest parts of human society, there was a
secret, though unjust, way among men, of indulging
the seeds of ill-nature and envy, by comparing their
own state of life to that of another, and grudging the

approach of their neighbour to their own happiness; and on the other side, he, who is the less at his ease, repines at the other, who he thinks has unjustly the advantage over him. Thus the civil and military lists look upon each other with much ill-nature; the soldier repines at the courtier's power, and the courtier rallies the soldier's honour; or, to come to lower instances, the private men in the horse and foot of an army, the carmen and coachmen in the city streets, mutually look upon each other with ill-will, when they are in competition for quarters, or the way in their respective motions.

"It is very well, good captain," interrupted Sir Andrew: "you may attempt to turn the discourse if you think fit; but I must, however, have a word or two with Sir Roger, who, I see, thinks he has paid me off, and been very severe upon the merchant. I shall not," continued he, "at this time remind Sir Roger of the great and noble monuments of charity and public spirit which have been erected by merchants since the Reformation, but at present content myself with what he allows us, parsimony and frugality. If it were consistent with the quality of so ancient a baronet as Sir Roger, to keep an account, or measure things by the most infallible way, that of numbers, he would prefer our parsimony to his hospitality. If to drink so many hogsheads is to be hospitable, we do not con-

tend for the fame of that virtue; but it would be
worth while to consider, whether so many artificers
at work ten days together by my appointment, or so
many peasants made merry on Sir Roger's charge,
are the men more obliged?   I believe the families of
the artificers will thank me more than the households
of the peasants shall Sir Roger.   Sir Roger gives to
his men; but I place mine above the necessity or
obligation of my bounty.   I am in very little pain for
the Roman proverb upon the Carthaginian traders;
the Romans were their professed enemies: I am only
sorry no Carthaginian histories have come to our
hands: we might have been taught perhaps by them
some proverbs against the Roman generosity, in
fighting for and bestowing other people's goods.   But
since Sir Roger has taken occasion from an old
proverb, to be out of humour with merchants, it
should be no offence to offer one not quite so old in
their defence,   When a man happens to break in
Holland, they say of him that 'He has not kept true
accounts.'   This phrase, perhaps among us, would
appear a soft or humorous way of speaking, but with
that exact nation it bears the highest reproach.   For a
man to be mistaken in the calculation of his expense,
in his ability to answer future demands, or to be im-
pertinently sanguine in putting his credit to too great
adventure, are all instances of as much infamy, as with

gayer nations to be failing in courage, or common honesty.

"Numbers are so much the measure of every thing that is valuable, that it is not possible to demonstrate the success of any action, or the prudence of any undertaking, without them. I say this in answer to what Sir Roger is pleased to say, 'that little that is truly noble can be expected from one who is ever poring on his cash-book, or balancing his accounts.' When I have my returns from abroad, I can tell to a shilling, by the help of numbers, the profit or loss by my adventure; but I ought also to be able to show that I had reason for making it, either from my own experience or that of other people, or from a reasonable presumption that my returns will be sufficient to answer my expense and hazard; and this is never to be done without the skill of numbers. For instance, if I am to trade to Turkey, I ought beforehand to know the demand of our manufactures there, as well as of their silks in England, and the customary prices that are given for both in each country. I ought to have a clear knowledge of these matters beforehand, that I may presume upon sufficient returns to answer the charge of the cargo I have fitted out, the freight and assurance out and home, the customs to the queen, and the interest of my own money; and, besides all these expenses, a reasonable profit to myself. Now what is there of scandal in this skill? What has the merchant done, that he should be so little in the good graces of Sir Roger? He throws down no man's enclosures, and tramples upon no man's corn; he takes nothing from the industrious labourer; he pays the poor man for his work; he communicates his profit with mankind; by the preparation of his cargo, and the manufacture of his returns, he furnishes employ- ment and subsistence to greater numbers than the richest nobleman; and even the nobleman is obliged to him for finding out foreign markets for the produce of his estate, and for making a great addition to his rents; and yet it is certain that none of all these things could be done by him without the exercise of his skill in numbers.

"This is the economy of the merchant; and the conduct of the gentleman must be the same, unless, by scorning to be the steward, he resolves the steward shall be the gentleman. The gentleman, no more than the merchant, is able, without the help of numbers, to account for the success of any action, or the prudence of any adventure. If, for instance, the chase is his whole adventure, his only returns must be the stag's horns in the great hall, and the fox's nose upon the stable door. Without doubt Sir Roger knows the full value of these returns; and if beforehand he had computed the charges of the chase, a gentleman of his discretion would certainly have hanged up all his dogs; he would never have brought back so many fine horses to the kennel; he would never have gone so often, like a blast, over fields of corn, If such, too, had been the conduct of all his ancestors, he might truly have boasted at this day, that the antiquity of his family had never been sullied by a trade ; a merchant had never been permitted with his whole estate to purchase a room for his picture in the gallery of the Coverley's, or to claim his descent from the maid of honour. But it is very happy for Sir Roger that the merchant paid so dear for his ambition. It is the misfortune of many other gentlemen to turn out of the seats of their ancestors, to make way for such new masters as have been more exact in their accounts' than themselves ; and certainly he deserves the estate a great deal better who has got it by his industry, than he who has lost it by his negligence."

SIR ROGER IN WESTMINSTER ABBEY

Ire tamen restat Numa quò devenit et Ancus.
HOR., *Epist.* i. 6, 27.

With Ancus, and with Numa, kings of Rome,
We must descend into the silent tomb.

My friend Sir Roger de Coverley told me the other
night that he had been reading my paper upon Westminster Abbey, in which, says he, there are a great
many ingenious fancies. He told me at the same time
that he observed I had promised another paper upon
the tombs, and that he should be glad to go and see
them with me, not having visited them since he had
read history. I could not at first imagine how this
came into the knight's head, till I recollected that he
had been very busy all last summer upon "Baker's
Chronicle," which he has quoted several times in his disputes with Sir Andrew Freeport since his last coming
to town. Accordingly I promised to call upon him the
next morning, that we might go together to the abbey.

I found the knight under his butler's hands, who
always shaves him. He was no sooner dressed than
he called for a glass of the widow Trueby's water,
which he told me he always drank before he went

abroad. He recommended to me a dram of it at the same time, with so much heartiness, that I could not forbear drinking it. As soon as I had got it down, I found it very unpalatable; upon which the knight, observing that I had made several wry faces, told me that he knew I should not like it at first, but that it was the best thing in the world against the stone or gravel.

I could have wished, indeed, that he had acquainted me with the virtues of it sooner; but it was too late to complain, and I knew what he had done was out of goodwill. Sir Roger told me further, that he looked upon it to be very good for a man whilst he staid in town, to keep off infection, and that he got together a quantity of it upon the first news of the sickness being at Dantzic: when, of a sudden, turning short to one of his servants, who stood behind him, he bid him call a hackney-coach, and take care it was an elderly man that drove it.

He then resumed his discourse upon Mrs. Trueby's water, telling me that the widow Trueby was one who did more good than all the doctors and apothecaries in the county: that she distilled every poppy that grew within five miles of her; that she distributed her water gratis among all sorts of people: to which the knight added, that she had a very great jointure, and that the whole country would fain have it a match

between him and her, "and truly," says Sir Roger,
"if I had not been engaged, perhaps I could not have
done better."

His discourse was broken off by his man's telling
him he had called a coach. Upon our going to it,
after having cast his eye upon the wheels, he asked the
coachman if his axle-tree was good; upon the fellow's
telling him he would warrant it, the knight turned to
me, told me he looked like an honest man, and went in
without further ceremony.

We had not gone far, when Sir Roger, popping out
his head, called the coachman down from his box, and
upon his presenting himself at the window, asked him
if he smoked. As I was considering what this would
end in, he bid him stop by the way at any good
tobacconist's, and take in a roll of their best Virginia.
Nothing material happened in the remaining part of
our journey, till we were set down at the west end of
the abbey.

As we went up the body of the church, the knight
pointed at the trophies upon one of the new monuments, and cried out, "A brave man, I warrant him!"
Passing afterwards by Sir Cloudsley Shovel, he flung
his hand that way, and cried, "Sir Cloudsley Shovel!
a very gallant man." As we stood before Busby's
tomb, the knight uttered himself again after the same
manner: "Dr. Busby! a great man: he whipped my

grandfather: a very great man! I should have gone to him myself, if I had not been a blockhead: a very great man!"

We were immediately conducted into the little chapel on the right hand. Sir Roger, planting himself at our historian's elbow, was very attentive to everything he said, particularly to the account he gave us of the lord who had cut off the King of Morocco's head. Among several other figures, he was very well pleased to see the statesman Cecil upon his knees; and, concluding them all to be great men, was conducted to the figure which represents that martyr to good housewifery who died by the prick of a needle. Upon our interpreter's telling us that she was a maid of honour to Queen Elizabeth, the knight was very inquisitive into her name and family; and, after having regarded her finger for some time, "I wonder," says he, "that Sir Richard Baker has said nothing of her in his 'Chronicle.'"

We were then conveyed to the two coronation chairs, where my old friend, after having heard that the stone underneath the most ancient of them, which was brought from Scotland, was called Jacob's pillow, sat himself down in the chair, and, looking like the figure of an old Gothic king, asked our interpreter what authority they had to say that Jacob had ever been in Scotland? The fellow, instead of returning

F—33

him an answer, told him that he hoped his honour would pay his forfeit. I could observe Sir Roger a little ruffled upon being thus trepanned; but our guide not insisting upon his demand, the knight soon recovered his good humour, and whispered in my ear, that if Will Wimble were with us, and saw those two chairs, it would go hard but he would get a tobacco-stopper out of one or t'other of them.

Sir Roger, in the next place, laid his hand upon Edward the Third's sword, and leaning upon the pommel of it, gave us the whole history of the Black Prince; concluding, that in Sir Richard Baker's opinion, Edward the Third was one of the greatest princes that ever sat upon the English throne.

We were then shown Edward the Confessor's tomb; upon which Sir Roger acquainted us, that he was the first who touched for the evil: and afterwards, Henry the Fourth's, upon which he shook his head, and told us there was fine reading in the casualties of that reign.

Our conductor then pointed to that monument where there is the figure of one of our English kings without a head; and upon giving us to know that the head, which was of beaten silver, had been stolen away several years since, "Some Whig, I'll warrant you," says Sir Roger; "you ought to lock up your kings better; they will carry off the body too if you don't take care."

The glorious names of Henry the Fifth and Queen Elizabeth gave the knight great opportunities of shining, and of doing justice to Sir Richard Baker, who, as our knight observed with some surprise, had a great many kings in him, whose monuments he had not seen in the abbey.

For my own part, I could not but be pleased to see the knight show such an honest passion for the glory of his country, and such a respectful gratitude to the memory of its princes.

I must not omit that the benevolence of my good old friend, which flows out towards every one he converses with, made him very kind to our interpreter, whom he looked upon as an extraordinary man : for which reason he shook him by the hand at parting, telling him that he should be very glad to see him at his lodgings in Norfolk Buildings, and talk over these matters with him more at leisure.

SIR ROGER AT THE PLAY

Respicere exemplar vitæ morumque jubebo
Doctum imitatorem, et veras hinc ducere voces.

                                    HOR., *Ars poet.* 317.

Keep Nature's great original in view,
And thence the living images pursue.   FRANCIS.

MY friend Sir Roger de Coverley, when we last met together at the club, told me that he had a great mind to see the new tragedy with me, assuring me, at the same time, that he had not been at a play these twenty years. "The last I saw," said Sir Roger, "was the Committee, which I should not have gone to neither, had not I been told beforehand, that it was a good Church of England comedy. He then proceeded to inquire of me, who this distressed mother was; and, upon hearing that she was Hector's widow, he told me that her husband was a brave man, and that, when he was a schoolboy, he had read his life at the end of the dictionary. My friend asked me, in the next place, if there would not be some danger in coming home late, in case the Mohocks should be abroad. "I assure you," says he, "I thought I had fallen into their hands last night; for I observed two or three lusty black men that followed me half-way up Fleet Street, and mended their pace behind me, in proportion as I put on to get away from them. You must know," continued the knight, with a smile, "I fancied they had a mind to hunt me; for I remember an honest gentleman in my neighbourhood who was served such a trick in King Charles the Second's time, for which reason he has not ventured himself in town ever since. I might have shown them very good sport, had this been their design; for, as I am an old fox-hunter, I should have turned and dodged and have played them a thousand tricks they had never seen in their lives before." Sir Roger added, that "if these gentlemen had any such intention, they did not succeed very well in it; for I threw them out," says he, "at the end of Norfolk Street, where I doubled the corner, and got shelter in my lodgings before they could imagine what was become of me. However," says the knight, "if Captain Sentry will make one with us to-morrow night, and if you will both of you call upon me about four o'clock, that we may be at the house before it is full, I will have my own coach in readiness to attend you, for John tells me he has got the fore-wheels mended."

The captain, who did not fail to meet me there at the appointed hour, bid Sir Roger fear nothing, for that he had put on the same sword which he made use of at the battle of Steenkirk. Sir Roger's servants, and, among the rest, my old friend the butler, had, I found, provided themselves with good oaken plants, to

attend their master upon this occasion.   When we had
placed him in his coach, with myself at his left-hand,
the captain before him, and his butler at the head of
his footmen in the rear, we convoyed him in safety to
the playhouse, where, having marched up the entry in
good order, the captain and I went in with him, and
seated him betwixt us in the pit.   As soon as the house
was full, and the candles lighted, my old friend stood
up, and looked about him with that pleasure which a
mind seasoned with humanity naturally feels in itself,
at the sight of a multitude of people who seem pleased
with one another and partake of the same common
entertainment.   I could not but fancy to myself, as the
old man stood up in the middle of the pit, that he made
a very proper centre to a tragic audience.   Upon the
entering of Pyrrhus, the knight told me that he did not
believe the King of France himself had a better strut.
I was indeed very attentive to my old friend's remarks,
because I looked upon them as a piece of natural
criticism, and was well pleased to hear him, at the conclusion of almost every scene, telling me that he could
not imagine how the play would end.   One while he
appeared much concerned for Andromache ; and, a little
while after, as much for Hermione ; and was extremely
puzzled to think what would become of Pyrrhus.

When Sir Roger saw Andromache's obstinate refusal
to her lover's importunities, he whispered me in the ear,

that he was sure she would never have him; to which he added, with a more than ordinary vehemence, "You can't imagine, sir, what it is to have to do with a widow." Upon Pyrrhus's threatening afterwards to leave her, the knight shook his head and muttered to himself, "Ay, do if you can." This part dwelt so much upon my friend's imagination, that at the close of the third act, as I was thinking of something else, he whispered me in my ear, " These widows, sir, are the most perverse creatures in the world. But pray," says he, "you that are a critic, is this play according to your dramatic rules, as you call them ? Should your people in tragedy always talk to be understood ? Why, there is not a single sentence in this play that I do not know the meaning of."

The fourth act very luckily began before I had time to give the old gentleman an answer. "Well," says the knight, sitting down with great satisfaction, "I suppose we are now to see Hector's ghost." He then renewed his attention, and, from time to time, fell a-praising the widow. He made indeed a little mistake as to one of her pages, whom, at his first entering, he took for Astyanax; but he quickly set himself right in that particular, though, at the same time, he owned he should have been very glad to have seen the little boy, who, says he, must needs be a very fine child by the account that is given of him. Upon Hermione's going off with a menace to Pyrrhus, the audience gave a loud clap, to which Sir Roger added, "On my word, a notable young baggage!"

As there was a very remarkable silence and stillness in the audience during the whole action, it was natural for them to take the opportunity of these intervals between the acts, to express their opinion of the players and of their respective parts. Sir Roger, hearing a cluster of them praise Orestes, struck in with them, and told them that he thought his friend Pylades was a very sensible man. As they were afterwards applauding Pyrrhus, Sir Roger put in a second time. "And let me tell you," says he, "though he speaks but little, I like the old fellow in whiskers as well as any of them." Captain Sentry seeing two or three wags who sat near us lean with an attentive ear towards Sir Roger, and fearing lest they should smoke the knight, plucked him by the elbow, and whispered something in his ear that lasted till the opening of the fifth act. The knight was wonderfully attentive to the account which Orestes gives of Pyrrhus's death, and at the conclusion of it, told me it was such a bloody piece of work that he was glad it was not done upon the stage. Seeing afterwards Orestes in his raving fit, he grew more than ordinarily serious, and took occasion to moralise, in his way, upon an evil conscience, adding, that Orestes in his madness looked as if he saw something.

As we were the first that came into the house, so we were the last that went out of it; being resolved to have a clear passage for our old friend, whom we did not care to venture among the justling of the crowd. Sir Roger went out fully satisfied with his entertainment, and we guarded him to his lodging in the same manner that we had brought him to the playhouse; being highly pleased for my own part, not only with the performance of the excellent piece which had been presented, but with the satisfaction which it had given to the good old man.

WILL HONEYCOMB AT THE CLUB

Torva leæna lupum sequitur, lupus ipse capellam :
Florentem cytisum sequitur lasciva capella.

VIRG., Ecl. ii. 63.

Lions the wolves, and wolves the kids pursue,
The kids sweet thyme—and still I follow you.

WARTON.

As we were at the club last night, I observed that my friend Sir Roger, contrary to his usual custom, sat very silent, and, instead of minding what was said by the company, was whistling to himself in a very thoughtful mood, and playing with a cork. 1 jogged Sir Andrew Freeport, who sat between us, and, as we

F*—33

were both observing him, we saw the knight shake his
head, and heard him say to himself, "A foolish woman!
I can't believe it." Sir Andrew gave him a gentle pat
upon the shoulder, and offered to lay him a bottle of
wine that he was thinking of the widow. My old
friend started, and, recovering out of his brown study,
told Sir Andrew that once in his life he had been in
the right. In short, after some little hesitation, Sir
Roger told us, in the fulness of his heart, that he had
just received a letter from his steward, which acquainted him that his old rival and antagonist in the
country, Sir David Dundrum, had been making a visit
to the widow. "However," says Sir Roger, "I can
never think that she'll have a man that's half a year
older than I am, and a noted republican into the
bargain."

Will Honeycomb, who looks upon love as his particular province, interrupting our friend with a jaunty
laugh, "I thought, knight," says he, " thou hadst lived
long enough in the world not to pin thy happiness upon
one that is a woman, and a widow. I think that,
without vanity, I may pretend to know as much of the
female world as any man in Great Britain; though the
chief of my knowledge consists in this, that they are
not to be known." Will immediately, with his usual
fluency, rambled into an account of his own amours.
"I am now," says he, "upon the verge of fifty."

though, by the way, we all knew he was turned of threescore. " You may easily guess," continued Will, "that I have not lived so long in the world without having had some thoughts of settling in it, as the phrase is. To tell you truly, I have several times tried my fortune that way, though I can't much boast of my success.

" I made my first addresses to a young lady in the country ; but, when I thought things were pretty well drawing to a conclusion, her father happening to hear that I had formerly boarded with a surgeon, the old put forbade me his house, and within a fortnight after married his daughter to a fox-hunter in the neighbourhood.

"I made my next applications to a widow, and attacked her so briskly, that I thought myself within a fortnight of her. As I waited upon her one morning, she told me that she intended to keep her ready-money and jointure in her own hand, and desired me to call upon her attorney in Lyon's-Inn, who would adjust with me what it was proper for me to add to it. I was so rebuffed by this overture, that 1 never inquired either for her or her attorney afterwards.

" A few months after, I addressed myself to a young lady who was an only daughter, and of a good family. I danced with her at several balls, squeezed her by the hand. said soft things to her, and, in short, made no doubt of her heart; and though my fortune was not equal to hers, I was in hopes that her fond father would not deny her the man she had fixed her affections upon. But as I went one day to the house, in order to break the matter to him, I found the whole family in confusion, and heard, to my unspeakable surprise, that Miss Jenny was that very morning run away with the butler.

" I then courted a second widow, and am at a loss to this day how I came to miss her, for she had often commended my person and behaviour. Her maid, indeed, told me one day that her mistress had said she never saw a gentleman with such a spindle pair of legs as Mr. Honeycomb.

" After this I laid siege to four heiresses succes· sively, and, being a handsome young dog in those days, quickly made a breach in their hearts ; but I don't know how it came to pass, though I seldom failed of getting the daughter's consent, I could never in my life get the old people on my side.

" I could give you an account of a thousand other unsuccessful attempts, particularly of one which I made some years since upon an old woman, whom I had certainly borne away with flying colours, if her relations had not come pouring in to her assistance from all parts of England ; nay, I believe I should have got her at last had not she been carried off by a hard frost."

As Will's transitions are extremely quick, he turned

from Sir Roger, and, applying himself to me, told me there was a passage in the book I had considered last Saturday which deserved to be writ in letters of gold; and, taking out a pocket Milton, read the following lines, which are part of one of Adam's speeches to Eve after the fall :—

> —Oh ! why did God,
> Creator wise ! that peopled highest heave
> With spirits masculine, create at last
> This novelty on earth, this fair defect
> Of nature, and not fill the world at once
> With men, as angels, without feminine ?
> Or find some other way to generate
> Mankind ?   This mischief had not then befallen,
> And more that shall befall ; innumerable
> Disturbances on earth, through female snares,
> And strait conjunction with this sex : for either
> He never shall find out fit mate, but such
> As some misfortune brings him, or mistake ;
> Or whom he wishes most shall seldom gain,
> Through her perverseness ; but shall see her gain'd
> By a far worse ; or, if she love, withheld
> By parents ; or his happiest choice too late
> Shall meet, already linked and wedlock-bound
> To a fell adversary, his hate or shame :
> Which infinite calamity shall cause
> To human life, and household peace confound.   x. 888.

Sir Roger listened to this passage with great attention, and, desiring Mr. Honeycomb to fold down a leaf at the place and lend him his book, the knight put it up in his pocket, and told us that he would read over those verses again before he went to bed.

WITH SIR ROGER TO SPRING GARDEN

Criminibus debent hortos.—

JUV., *Sat.* i. 75.

A beauteous garden, but by vice maintain'd.

As I was sitting in my chamber, and thinking on a subject for my next Spectator, I heard two or three irregular bounces at my landlady's door, and upon the opening of it, a loud cheerful voice inquiring whether the philosopher was at home. The child who went to the door answered very innocently that he did not lodge there. I immediately recollected that it was my good friend Sir Roger's voice; and that I had promised to go with him on the water to Spring Garden, in case it proved a good evening. The knight put me in mind of my promise from the bottom of the staircase, but told me, that if I was speculating he would stay below till I had done. Upon my coming down, I found all the children of the family got about my old friend; and my landlady herself, who is a notable prating gossip, engaged in a conference with him; being mightily pleased with his stroking her little boy upon the head. and bidding him be a good child and mind his book.

We were no sooner come to the Temple Stairs, but

we were surrounded with a crowd of watermen, offering us their respective services. Sir Roger, after having looked about him very attentively, spied one with a wooden leg, and immediately gave him orders to get his boat ready. As we were walking towards it, " You must know," says Sir Roger, " I never make use of anybody to row me that has not either lost a leg or an arm. I would rather bate him a few strokes of his oar than not employ an honest man that has been wounded in the queen's service. If I was a lord or a bishop, and kept a barge, I would not put a fellow in my livery that had not a wooden leg."

My old friend, after having seated himself, and trimmed the boat with his coachman, who, being a very sober man, always serves for ballast on these occasions, we made the best of our way for Vauxhall. Sir Roger obliged the waterman to give us the history of his right leg ; and, hearing that he had left it at La Hogue, with many particulars which passed in that glorious action, the knight, in the triumph of his heart, made several reflections on the greatness of the British nation ;. as, that one Englishman could beat three Frenchmen ; that we could never be in danger of popery so long as we took care of our fleet ; that the Thames was the noblest river in Europe ; that London Bridge was a greater piece of work than any of the seven wonders of the world ; with many other honest prejudices which naturally cleave to the heart of a true Englishman.

After some short pause, the old knight turning about his head twice or thrice, to take a survey of this great metropolis, bid me observe how thick the city was set with churches, and that there was scarce a single steeple on this side Temple Bar. " A most heathenish sight !" says Sir Roger : "there is no religion at this end of the town. The fifty new churches will very much amend the prospect ; but church work is slow, church work is slow."

I do not remember I have any where mentioned in Sir Roger's character, his custom of saluting every body that passes by him with a good morrow, or a good night. This the old man does out of the overflowings of his humanity ; though, at the same time, it renders him so popular among all his country neighbours, that it is thought to have gone a good way in making him once or twice knight of the shire. He cannot forbear this exercise of benevolence even in town, when he meets with any one in his morning or evening walk. It broke from him to several boats that passed by us upon the water ; but, to the knight's great surprise, as he gave the good night to two or three young fellows a little before our landing, one of them, instead of returning the civility, asked us what queer old put we had in the boat, and whether he was not ashamed to go a-wenching at his years; with a great deal of the like Thames ribaldry. Sir Roger seemed a little shocked at first, but at length assuming a face of magistracy, told us, that if he were a Middlesex justice, he would make such vagrants know that her Majesty's subjects were no more to be abused by water than by land.

We were now arrived at Spring Garden, which is excellently pleasant at this time of the year. When I considered the fragrancy of the walks and bowers, with the choirs of birds that sung upon the trees, and the loose tribe of people that walked under their shades, I could not but look upon the place as a kind of Mahometan paradise. Sir Roger told me it put him in mind of a little coppice by his house in the country, which his chaplain used to call an aviary of nightingales. "You must understand," says the knight, "there is nothing in the world that pleases a man in love so much as your nightingale. Ah, Mr. Spectator, the many moonlight nights that I have walked by myself, and thought on the widow by the music of the nightingale!" He here fetched a deep sigh, and was falling into a fit of musing, when a mask, who came behind him, gave him a gentle tap upon the shoulder and asked him if he would drink a bottle of mead with her? But the knight being startled at so unexpected a familiarity, and displeased to be interrupted in his thoughts of the widow, told her "she was a wanton baggage;" and bid her go about her business.

We concluded our walk with a glass of Burton ale, and a slice of hung beef. When we had done eating ourselves, the knight called a waiter to him, and bid him carry the remainder to a waterman that had but one leg. I perceived the fellow stared upon him at the oddness of the message, and was going to be saucy; upon which I ratified the knight's commands with a peremptory look.

As we were going out of the garden, my old friend thinking himself obliged, as a member of the quorum, to animadvert upon the morals of the place, told the mistress of the house, who sat at the bar, that he should be a better customer to her garden, if there were more nightingales, and fewer strumpets.

SIR ROGER'S DEATH

Heu pietas ! heu prisca fides !—
                                   VIRG., *Æn.* vi. 878.

Mirror of ancient faith !—
Undaunted worth ! Inviolable truth !
                                   DRYDEN.

WE last night received a piece of ill-news at our club which very sensibly afflicted every one of us. I question not but my readers themselves will be troubled at the hearing of it. To keep them no longer in suspense, Sir Roger de Coverley is dead. He departed this life at his house in the country, after a few weeks' sickness. Sir Andrew Freeport has a letter from one of his correspondents in those parts, that informs him the old man caught a cold at the county sessions, as he was very warmly promoting an address of his own penning, in which he succeeded according to his wishes. But this particular comes from a whig justice of peace, who was always Sir Roger's enemy and antagonist. I have letters both from the chaplain and Captain Sentry, which mention nothing of it, but are filled with many particulars to the honour of the good old man. I have likewise a letter from the butler, who took so much care of me last summer when I was at the knight's house. As my friend the butler mentions, in the simplicity of his heart, several circumstances the others have passed over in silence, I shall give my reader a copy of his letter, without any alteration or diminution.

"HONOURED SIR,—Knowing that you was my old master's good friend, I could not forbear sending you the melancholy news of his death, which has afflicted the whole country, as well as his poor servants, who loved him. I may say, better than we did our lives. I

am afraid he caught his death the last county-sessions,
where he would go to see justice done to a poor widow
woman, and her fatherless children, that had been
wronged by a neighbouring gentleman; for you know,
sir, my good master was always the poor man's
friend. Upon his coming home, the first complaint he
made was, that he had lost his roast-beef stomach,
not being able to touch a sirloin, which was served up
according to custom; and you know he used to take
great delight in it. From that time forward he grew
worse and worse, but still kept a good heart to the last.
Indeed, we were once in great hopes of his recovery,
upon a kind message that was sent him from the
widow lady whom he had made love to the forty last
years of his life; but this only proved a lightning
before death. He has bequeathed to this lady, as a
token of his love, a great pearl necklace, and a couple
of silver bracelets set with jewels, which belonged to
my good old lady his mother. He has bequeathed the
fine white gelding that he used to ride a hunting upon
to his chaplain, because he thought he would be kind
to him; and has left you all his books. He has,
moreover, bequeathed to the chaplain a very pretty
tenement with good lands about it. It being a very
cold day when he made his will, he left for mourning
to every man in the parish, a great frieze-coat, and to
every woman a black riding hood. It was a most

moving sight to see him take leave of his poor servants, commending us all for our fidelity, whilst we were not able to speak a word for weeping. As we most of us are grown grayheaded in our dear master's service, he has left us pensions and legacies, which we may live very comfortably upon the remaining part of our days. He has bequeathed a great deal more in charity, which is not yet come to my knowledge, and it is peremptorily said in the parish that he has left money to build a steeple to the church: for he was heard to say some time ago, that, if he lived two years longer, Coverley church should have a steeple to it. The chaplain tells everybody that he made a very good end, and never speaks of him without tears. He was buried, according to his own directions, among the family of the Coverleys, on the left hand of his father Sir Arthur. The coffin was carried by six of his tenants, and the pall held up by six of the quorum. The whole parish followed the corpse with heavy hearts, and in their mourning suits; the men in frieze, and the women in riding-hoods. Captain Sentry, my master's nephew, has taken possession of the Hall-house, and the whole estate. When my old master saw him a little before his death, he shook him by the hand, and wished him joy of the estate which was falling to him, desiring him only to make a good use of it, and to pay the several legacies. and the gifts of

charity, which he told him he had left as quit-rents
upon the estate. The captain truly seems a courteous
man, though he says but little. He makes much of
those whom my master loved, and shows great kindness to the old house-dog, that you know my poor
master was so fond of. It would have gone to your
heart to have heard the moans the dumb creature
made on the day of my master's death. He has never
enjoyed himself since ; no more has any of us. It was
the melancholiest day for the poor people that ever
happened in Worcestershire. This being all from,

" Honoured sir,

" Your most sorrowful servant,

" Edward Biscuit.

"P.S.—My master desired, some weeks before he
died, that a book, which comes to you by the carrier,
should be given to Sir Andrew Freeport in his
name."

This letter, notwithstanding the poor butler's manner of writing it, gave us such an idea of our good
old friend, that upon the reading of it there was not
a dry eye in the club. Sir Andrew, opening the
book, found it to be a collection of acts of parliament.
There was in particular the Act of Uniformity, with
some passages in it marked by Sir Roger's own hand.
Sir Andrew found that they related to two or three

points which he had disputed with Sir Roger, the last time he appeared at the club. Sir Andrew, who would have been merry at such an incident on another occasion, at the sight of the old man's hand-writing burst into tears, and put the book into his pocket. Captain Sentry informs me that the knight has left rings and mourning for every one in the club.

WILL HONEYCOMB'S MARRIAGE

Sic visum Veneri ; cui placet impares
Formas atque animos sub juga ahenea
Sævo mittere cum joco.

HOR. *Car.* i. 33, 10.

Thus Venus sports : the rich, the base,
Unlike in fortune and in face,
To disagreeing love provokes ;
    When cruelly jocose,
    She ties the fatal noose,
And binds unequals to the brazen yokes.

CREECH.

IT is very usual for those who have been severe upon marriage in some part or other of their lives, to enter into the fraternity which they have ridiculed, and to see their raillery return upon their own heads. I scarce

ever knew a woman-hater that did not, sooner or later
pay for it. Marriage, which is a blessing to another
man, falls upon such an one as a judgment. Mr.
Congreve's Old Bachelor is set forth to us with much
wit and humour, as an example of this kind. In
short, those who have most distinguished themselves
by railing at the sex in general, very often make an
honourable amends, by choosing one of the most worth-
less persons of it for a companion and yoke-fellow.
Hymen takes his revenge in kind on those who turn his
mysteries into ridicule.

My friend Will Honeycomb, who was so unmercifully
witty upon the women in a couple of letters which I
lately communicated to the public, has given the ladies
ample satisfaction by marrying a farmer's daughter ;
a piece of news which came to our club by the last
post. The templar is very positive that he has married
a dairy-maid ; but Will, in his letter to me on this
occasion, sets the best face upon the matter that he can,
and gives a more tolerable account of his spouse. I
must confess I suspected something more than ordinary,
when, upon opening the letter, I found that Will was
fallen off from his former gaiety, having changed
" Dear Spec," which was his usual salute at the begin-
ning of the letter, into " My worthy friend," and sub-
scribed himself in the latter end of it in full length
William Honeycomb. In short, the gay, the loud, the

vain Will Honeycomb, who had made love to every great fortune that has appeared in town for about thirty years together, and boasted of favours from ladies whom he had never seen, is at length wedded to a plain country girl.

His letter gives us the picture of a converted rake. The sober character of the husband is dashed with the man of the town, and enlivened with those little cant phrases, which have made my friend Will often thought very pretty company. But let us hear what he says for himself.

"MY WORTHY FRIEND,

"I question not but you, and the rest of my acquaintance, wonder that I, who have lived in the smoke and gallantries of the town for thirty years together, should all on a sudden grow fond of a country life. Had not my dog of a steward ran away as he did without making up his accounts, I had still been immersed in sin and sea-coal. But since my late forced visit to my estate, I am so pleased with it, that I am resolved to live and die upon it. I am every day abroad among my acres, and can scarce forbear filling my letter with breezes, shades, flowers, meadows, and purling streams. The simplicity of manners, which I have heard you so often speak of, and which appears here in perfection, charms me wonderfully. As an

instance of it I must acquaint you, and by your means
the whole club, that I have lately married one of my
tenant's daughters. She is born of honest parents;
and though she has no portion, she has a great deal of
virtue. The natural sweetness and innocence of her
behaviour, the freshness of her complexion, the unaffected turn of her shape and person, shot me through
and through every time I saw her, and did more execu-
tion upon me in grogram, than the greatest beauty in
town or court had ever done in brocade. In short, she
is such a one as promises me a good heir to my estate;
and if by her means I cannot leave to my children what
are falsely called the gifts of birth, high titles, and
alliances, I hope to convey to them the more real and
valuable gifts of birth—strong bodies, and healthy
constitutions. As for your fine women, I need not tell
thee that I know them. I have had my share in their
graces; but no more of that. It shall be my business
hereafter to live the life of an honest man, and to act
as becomes the master of a family. I question not but
I shall draw upon me the raillery of the town, and be
treated to the tune of 'The Marriage-hater Matched;'
but I am prepared for it. I have been as witty upon
others in my time. To tell thee truly, I saw such a
tribe of fashionable young fluttering coxcombs shot up
that I did not think my post of an *homme de ruelle* any
longer tenable. I felt a certain stiffness in my limbs,

which entirely destroyed that jauntiness of air I was once master of. Besides, for I may now confess my age to thee, I have been eight-and-forty above these twelve years. Since my retirement into the country will make a vacancy in the club, I could wish you would fill up my place with my friend Tom Dapperwit. He has an infinite deal of fire, and knows the town. For my own part, as I have said before, I shall endeavour to live hereafter suitable to a man in my station, as a prudent head of a family, a good husband, a careful father, when it shall so happen, and as

"Your most sincere friend

"and humble servant,

"WILLIAM HONEYCOMB."

THE CLUB DISSOLVED

Quamvis digressu veteris confusus amici,
Laudo tamen. JUV., *Sat.* iii. 1.

Though grieved at the departure of my friend,
His purpose of retiring I commend.

I BELIEVE most people begin the world with a resolution to withdraw from it into a serious kind of solitude or retirement when they have made themselves easy in it. Our unhappiness is that we find out some excuse or other for deferring such our good resolutions till our intended retreat is cut off by death. But among all kinds of people there are none who are so hard to part with the world as those who are grown old in the heaping up of riches. Their minds are so warped with their constant attention to gain, that it is very difficult for them to give their souls another bent, and convert them towards those objects, which, though they are proper for every stage of life, are so more especially for the last. Horace describes an old usurer as so charmed with the pleasures of a country life that in order to make a purchase he called in all his money; but what was the event of it? Why, in a very few days after he put it out again. I am engaged in this series of thought by a discourse which I had last week with my worthy friend, Sir Andrew Freeport, a man of so much natural eloquence, good sense, and probity of mind, that I always hear him with a particular pleasure. As we were sitting together, being the sole remaining members of our club, Sir Andrew gave me an account of the many busy scenes of life in which he had been engaged, and, at the same time, reckoned up to me abundance of those lucky hits, which at another time he would have called pieces of good fortune; but in the temper of mind he was then, he termed them mercies, favours of Providence, and blessings upon an honest industry. "Now," says he, "you must know, my good friend, I am so used to consider myself as creditor and debtor, that I often state my accounts after the same manner with regard to heaven and my own soul. In this case, when I look upon the debtor side, I find such innumerable articles that I want arithmetic to cast them up; but when I look upon the creditor side, I find little more than blank paper. Now, though I am very well satisfied that it is not in my power to balance accounts with my Maker, I am resolved, however, to turn all my future endeavours that way. You must not therefore be surprised, my friend, if you hear that I am betaking myself to a more thoughtful kind of life, and if I meet you no more in this place."

I could not but approve so good a resolution, notwithstanding the loss I shall suffer by it. Sir Andrew has since explained himself to me more at large in the following letter, which is just come to my hands :—

"GOOD MR. SPECTATOR,

"Notwithstanding my friends at the club have always rallied me when I have talked of retiring from business, and repeated to me one of my own sayings, that "a merchant has never enough till he has got a little more," I can now inform you, that there is one in the world who thinks he has enough, and is determined to pass the remainder of his life in the enjoy-

ment of what he has. You know me so well that I
need not tell you I mean by the enjoyment of my pos-
sessions the making of them useful to the public. As
the greatest part of my estate has been hitherto of an
unsteady and volatile nature, either tossed upon seas or
fluctuating in funds, it is now fixed and settled in
substantial acres and tenements. I have removed it
from the uncertainty of stocks, winds, and waves, and
disposed of it in a considerable purchase. This will
give me great opportunity of being charitable in my
way, that is, in setting my poor neighbours to work,
and giving them a comfortable subsistence out of their
own industry. My gardens, my fish-ponds, my arable
and pasture grounds, shall be my several hospitals, or
rather workhouses, in which I propose to maintain a
great many indigent persons, who are now starving in
my neighbourhood. I have got a fine spread of im-
provable lands, and in my own thoughts am already
ploughing up some of them, fencing others, planting
woods, and draining marshes. In fine, as I have my
share in the surface of this island, I am resolved to
make it as beautiful a spot as any in her Majesty's
dominions; at least there is not an inch of it which
shall not be cultivated to the best advantage, and do
its utmost for its owner. As in my mercantile employment I so disposed of my affairs, that, from whatever corner of the compass the wind blew it was

bringing home one or other of my ships, I hope as a husbandman to contrive it so, that not a shower of rain, or a glimpse of sunshine shall fall upon my estate without bettering some part of it, and contributing to the products of the season. You know it has been hitherto my opinion of life, that it is thrown away when it is not some way useful to others. But when I am riding out by myself, in the fresh air on the open heath that lies by my house, I find several other thoughts growing up in me. I am now of opinion that a man of my age may find business enough on himself, by setting his mind in order, preparing it for another world, and reconciling it to the thoughts of death. I must, therefore, acquaint you, that besides those usual methods of charity, of which I have before spoken, I am at this very instant finding out a convenient place where I may build an almshouse, which I intend to endow very handsomely, for a dozen superannuated husbandmen. It will be a great pleasure to me to say my prayers twice a day with men of my own years, who all of them, as well as myself, may have their thoughts taken up how they shall die, rather than how they shall live. I remember an excellent saying that I learned at school, "*Finis coronat opus*" You know best whether it be in Virgil or in Horace; it is my business to apply it. If your affairs will permit you to take the country air with me sometimes, you shall

find an apartment fitted up for you, and shall be every
day entertained with beef or mutton of my own feeding,
fish out of my own ponds, and fruit out of my own
gardens.   You shall have free egress and regress about
my house, without having any questions asked you;
and, in a word, such a hearty welcome as you may
expect from

       " Your most sincere friend

           " and humble servant,

              " ANDREW FREEPORT."

Printed by CASSELL & COMPANY, LIMITED, La Belle Sauvage, London E.C.
30.608

Made in the USA
Lexington, KY
20 September 2012